The Scribbleis of Brevard
Christmas Anthology 2022

Published by The Scribblers of Brevard, Florida,
United States of America, 2022

ISBN: 9798369738948
Imprint: Independently Published

Available from Amazon Books in Paperback and the Amazon Kindle Bookstore.

Introduction

The Scribblers of Brevard is a long-standing group of writers who are based in Brevard County, Florida. The group has been publishing anthologies of their writings for several decades.

In that tradition, we are delighted to present the second edition of our Christmas-themed anthology. The original version in 2021 was a beautiful, slim gift that could be given at Christmas, but stay long on the shelf and in the heart and mind of its recipient and be read and re-read constantly. This updated, 2022 version contains all the original content but has over one hundred extra pages of new content added.

It features our famous fifty-word mini sagas, poetry, and short stories. When we think of a 'saga' we might initially think of a highly dramatic situation, but we want you to think of the punch that has to be packed into so few words.

These power-packed mini-stories are the equivalent of the poetic haiku – with a universal meaning that stays with you long after you have finished reading. We are indebted to one of our long-standing members, Nancy Clark, who pioneered the use of the fifty-word mini saga, in our group.

Our first edition was very well received by friends, family and readers far and wide and we think that this second edition will prove to be even more enjoyable. It would make the perfect Christmas gift and will still, just about, despite its additional 'girth,' fit into the Christmas stocking.

There is something for everyone in this collection. It's a unique pot-pourri of ideas, styles and approaches to the concept of Christmas, which often place family, home and friendship as relatable themes at their core but there are also many deviations from this traditional perspective - sometimes poignantly sad and frequently, absurdly comic – but always sharing a thought-provoking and insightful message.

Happy Christmas 2022 to all our readers!!

Dedication

This book is dedicated to my friend Elise, who lives here in Brevard County, Florida. She gathers, cooks and delivers food to the homeless, several days of the week, every week of every year. She canvasses a lot of left-over food from local stores but she also buys her own. Some nights, she doesn't get home till the early hours. It is not unusual for her to hand out over one hundred meals. At Christmas she gives out special goody bags, that she makes up herself, so that the homeless have some sort of a Christmas too.

Contents

Poetry

Short Stories and Memoirs

Author Biographies

50 Word Christmas Mini Sagas

Miracles

Richard McNamara

The tiny twinkling tree lights made reflections that danced on the walls. Suddenly there was electricity in the air that only lasted a second. The small face peering through the banister was astonished at the empty plate, empty glass, and the presents that had magically appeared under the tree.

The Christmas Run

Richard McNamara

Seven a.m., thirty-four degrees, thermal underwear, dirty jeans, leather chaps, and jacket. The oil was like sludge; not letting the big engine start. Ten kicks, and I'm on the road. I'm used to the gawks, but this morning is different. Maybe it's the wrapped present tied to the sissy bar.

Puppies

Richard McNamara

A quick nap curled up on the couch with the new puppy. A low growling noise wakes you up to a scene of utter destruction. Wrapping paper and ribbon everywhere, part of a shoe here, pieces of a shirt there, all enhanced by the familiar smell of your favorite cologne.

Xmas Surprise

Richard McNamara

Baby's second Christmas. What to buy? Asking baby, "What do you want for Christmas?" "I want this and this and this." It's Christmas morning. The toys are piled under the tree. Baby looks at the gifts and walks to the coffee table and picks up a roll of masking tape.

Christmas Joy

Richard McNamara

Christmas Eve. The mad dash to K-Mart and Sears to retrieve presents. The inevitable fight to get the kids to sleep. Finally, it's time. The grandparents get their gifts, and we get ours. Christmas morning and the sight of the kids attacking the pile of presents makes it all worthwhile.

No Respect

Richard McNamara

For weeks we ask, "What do you want for
Christmas?" Finally, we get a note—
"Everything in the Sears toy section
between pages 432 and 1127."
      "Could you be more specific?"
      "No," from the youngest.
      "We'll have to talk with Santa."
      "You do that."
      "Why you little . . ."

There's No Going Back Now

Richard McNamara

It's 4:30 AM Christmas morning. My father and I are assembling a desk. The instructions say, "Attach part C to part B with screws W." Part B has no holes for the screws! I grab the drill and bits from my toolbox and start drilling. God, I hope this works.

Tiny Dancer

Linda Paul

Following the Barbra Streisand impersonator, John took the stage; his short, chubby body gyrating to "Little Saint Nick." He hopped and twirled joyously; the Santa suit straining against his round belly. "Ho-ho-ho!" he laughed, as he yanked off the breakaway suit; his boxers flashing bright red and green Christmas lights.

A Christmas Divorce

By Linda Paul

"What did Jim get you for Christmas?" his niece asked. My husband's large family was gathered for Boxing Day at my in-laws' home. "Nothing," I replied. Her eyes widened in surprise. "Nothing. I won't be around here much longer. I don't care if you tell everybody here, I said that."

Christmas Concert

By Linda Paul

On Christmas morning we met in the icy parking lot. There were only six of us, but it was enough. Inside we stamped our snowy boots and unpacked our ukuleles. We sang familiar carols as some sat sleeping, some kept time and a woman with Alzheimer's stood to sing along.

The Last Time I Saw Bill

By Linda Paul

The last time I saw Bill was Christmas Eve 1968. I was stranded in the church parking lot. He offered me a ride. We'd broken up the year before. He'd said he "could do better" than me. This Christmas Eve he said I looked beautiful. I didn't care at all.

German Christmas

By Linda Paul

Christmas in Germany is quiet, white lights sparkling in the shop windows and decorating trees throughout the Fußgängerzonen. It is visiting the Weihnachtsmarkts for handmade presents and decorations. It's sitting in the cold with a handsome soldier and a Glühwein watching the shoppers stroll by. It's the opposite of Black Friday.

Christmas in the Desert

Louis Kicha

Outside, the temperature was eighty degrees in the north African desert. Inside, the barracks were air conditioned. A tiny artificial tree from home was decorated with insignia, cutouts from cards and topped with a paper star, a bottle of scotch at the base. This was Christmas in Libya, December 1969.

Christmas Engagement Ring

Louis Kicha

Last present was a small box. Inside was a ring made from florist wire and three tiny plastic carrots. She was not amused! My father said, "I hope there's more." I grinned, "I got this." I gave her another small box, the REAL ring. She was happy. Christmas was saved!

Mrs. Claus Saves Christmas

Carolyn Newby

Santa had a fever. Mrs. Claus scolded, "You've got that covid thing. Went snooping to see who was naughty or nice." Mrs. filled the sleigh with toys, hitched up the reindeer, and away they went. She hated chimney soot. Good job. Now they'd ride the sleigh to Anchorage for tests.

Christmas Hiding

Christopher Robin Adams

The Merritt Island forest was typical early-Florida: oak, palmetto, pine, scrub oak. One could hide without fear of discovery. Especially a small one. Movement would rattle low leaves, scare rabbits. He stood still. Then the yell. Loud. Closer. "I see a perfect tree, dad! This one!" Damn. They found me.

Age and Memory and Missing

Christopher Robin Adams

I was gonna tell you guys about a great TV movie that pops up every December. I can tell you some really great parts that will induce you to watch it. However, I just cannot remember the name. While I'm working on recall, let me tell you A Christmas Story.

My Father and I in a Time Far Away

Christopher Robin Adams

No lagoon. No environment. The Banana River meandered... somewhere. We stood in muck as a beer bottle bobbed in sunset-red water. I shouldered the new .22 rifle, carefully aimed, == bang! == and the bottle shattered to sink into mud. The bullet ended in a stump across the river. "Good shot, son."

Christmas

Nancy Clark

Molly sat by the fire, early Christmas morning, reminiscing about past Christmases in the house; filled with happiness. Today it was quiet. Her children all grown, with their own families, far away. The doorbell rang, she went to answer it. Her entire family stood before her. Shouting, "Surprise, Merry Christmas!"

Bygone Christmas

Nancy Clark

I wasn't ever able to experience a real Christmas tree. I was allergic to pine trees. We did have a beautiful, shiny, aluminum tree. I loved the way it sparkled and shimmered in spot lights. The Christmas balls matched the color of the lights each year. It was truly amazing.

Covid Christmas 2020

Nancy Clark

Christmas 2020, the sun is out and it's a brisk 44 degrees. Our plans for the day, meet the family at a local park to celebrate, the only way to be together for this special day and be safe. We may freeze our butts off, but at least we're together.

Holidays

Nancy Clark

Thanksgiving just passed and another year is almost at an end. Holidays just aren't the same anymore. I miss having my dad around to celebrate with us. Thanksgiving was one of his favorites. After all he could eat as much as he wanted, especially desserts; he wanted one of 'eachahs'!

Salty Tears

Nancy Clark

Salty tears ran down Sally's face. These were not tears of unhappiness. The tears were joyful, she had her last Covid shot and found out all her family had theirs. This was going to be a blessed holiday season compared to last year's. The family would be together to celebrate!

Christmas Wish

Nancy Clark

The Merriweather's recently moved to Florida. Cassie asked her parents would it snow. They shook their heads no. Tears ran down her face. She sobbed, "but, we always have a white Christmas! All I wish for is to have snow." Dad planned in advance, he had bought a snow machine!

Bah Humbug

Nancy Clark

The weatherman predicted no snow. You can't have Christmas without snow! It was cold enough to snow, so where was it! Susie kept tried to keep busy so she'd stop thinking about no snow for Christmas. Bedtime came finally. The next morning Susie woke up to find her white Christmas.

Christmas 2021

Nancy Clark

It's a new year and this one alive with love and laughter inside! No meeting outdoors to celebrate as we froze last year. We'll be warm and comfortable celebrating in our daughter's house, with Christmas wrap all over and delightful smells of dinner in the oven. Such a joyous feeling!

Christmas For The Birds

Nancy Clark

"Mom, the tree out front is sad," Susie said quietly. "Why is it sad?" "Cause it's bare. Can we put something on it for the birds?" "Sure, let's make popcorn and some peanut butter seed balls." Together they decorated all of the little trees with delightful treats for the birds.

Zoom Christmas 2020

Anne-Marie Derouault

No travel this year to faraway places. Only an invisible bridge. We were safe. Everyone shared: games, stories, pictures. We felt separate yet intimate. The greatest gift was when my mother, 91, told me later that she felt we did have Christmas together this year, different but a real one.

Christmas Night

Gloria I Colache

The scent wafting through the kitchen mixes with the fresh pine of the Christmas tree. Outside, the wind revolves around the lights. Our eyes are ablaze. We sing and toast each other with eggnog. It moves the heart, wishing if only all the family were here. Merry Christmas to everyone.

Your First Christmas

Gloria I Colache

The first sound you made was when the river of blood flowed but before that your first lullaby was the tick of your heart for nine months. Now, when you open the door, I smell the aromas of cinnamon and fresh pine and I recall my first Christmas with you.

The Christmas Play
Norbury Hall Junior School 1961

Elayne Kershaw

The lights go down. The curtains swish open. Year One is crammed onto the stage, giggling, and shuffling their feet. Cue Silent Night! Joseph sings a shaky first line A Capello. Mary cradles baby Jesus without dropping him. Three wise men bow down displaying their bottoms, inadvertently, to thunderous applause.

Christmas Eve 1965

Elayne Kershaw

The milk and carrots are ready for the reindeer. The Christmas tree lights illuminate the path to my empty, expectant sack. I count thousands of sheep. At long last he comes. Through squinted eye I discover that my dad is Father Christmas. This is the best present in the world.

**Cooking for Christmas
Marple Hall Grammar School for Girls 1969**

Elayne Kershaw

Chocolate log. Bake the sponge in a rectangular tin lined with greaseproof paper. Make the chocolate buttercream and the fondant icing. Fill, roll and top the cake with seasonal decorations. Clean the bowls with a large spoon, lick the sides and transfer to mouth. Throw up on the school bus.

Christmas Lost 1970

Elayne Kershaw

My mother has joined a sect. Christmas is cancelled because it was the feast of the Roman God Saturnalia, adopted by the early Christians. We knock on the doors of the uneducated to spread this revelation. Through candlelit windows, I glimpse fat, roasted turkey, and plum pudding. My mouth waters.

Christmas Restored 1977

Elayne Kershaw

My father brandishing the carving knife. My stepmother's hips swaying as she sashays the turkey over to the table. My grandad telling his stories. My nanna listening to them, again. My daughter, still enthralled by her early morning encounter with Father Christmas, waving a cracker in my face. Happy Christmas!

Christmas Eve 1995

Elayne Kershaw

It's nearly midnight. My eldest son is still awake. I kiss his forehead. He gazes at me in the dark. "Mum," he says, "It's ok. I know that Father Christmas isn't real." He looks over at his brothers. "But I won't tell them." They sleep soundly, wrapped still in magic.

New Year's Eve, Cheshire 2012
Minus Five Degrees at Midnight

Elayne Kershaw

"Let's toast chestnuts and drink champagne in the garden," I suggest. Blanket-wrapped, marvelling at the show hosted by the moon and the stars, I want to share this moment with our slumbering neighbours. "Where is your Christmas Spirit?" I shout. Suddenly our street is ablaze with a million, angry lights.

Christmas Dinner 2019

Elayne Kershaw

I am an orphan at the head of the table, holding the carving knife. My children have rejoined the nest. Too soon, they will kiss my cheek lovingly before dispersing across the country. I drop thin slices of turkey into the open, waiting mouths of my two cats. My babies.

Not So Merry

Peggy Downey Ball

Little beagle and I are delivering Christmas cookies next door. Treats are offered. Little beagle jumps happily. I open door to leave. Another visitor is arriving with his dog. Pit bull lunges. Beagle on floor, belly up. Owner pulls his dog off, but beagle is badly hurt. Christmas eve, euthanasia.

A Story of Real Love

Peggy Downey Ball

Beautiful young Mary was engaged to be married. When her fiancé learned she was pregnant, he knew the baby wasn't his and didn't want to marry her. But Mary was such a dear, special person, he decided to marry her anyway. That is how Joseph became the stepfather of Jesus.

The Sing-Along

Peggy Downey Ball

Having lost her job, Martha was depressed. She had promised to play piano for the nursing home's Christmas sing-along. Now, she wondered, could she bring anyone cheer? She fingered the keys: "Silent Night." The old voices rose with the music. Suddenly, hope was in the air and in Martha's heart.

Benny's Magical Christmas

Peggy Downey Ball

Benny gazed at figures in the creche under the tree. Strangely, his bare feet felt straw under them. Someone said, "Come, see the newborn king." Benny said, "I have no gift." Someone answered, "Then sing." Benny's mouth opened; words came out: "Oh, Holy Night." A song he had never heard.

Christmas is Saved

Peggy Insula

Rudolph awoke from a Christmas Eve nap. His head ached; his nose was stuffy; he had a hacking cough. Santa paced back and forth in the barn. "Christmas is ruined!" he cried. An elf scurried to the medicine cabinet and brought Rudolph a mega-gulp of Robitussin. Rudolph led the sleigh!

Holy Night

Peggy Insula

Bright stars glittered in the frosty night. A star more brilliant than all the rest beamed rays on shivering shepherds and kissed a cave in Bethlehem. Inside, cattle and sheep surrounded a road-weary couple until, breaking the awed stillness, a newborn baby cried. Angels sang, "Christ is born! Glorify Him!"

Clause

Nick Kaplan

Santa Clause, finishing his rum runner, harnesses his gators and manatee to the modified tiki raft. Grabbing his bag of presents, he dons his straw hat, flip-flops, sunglasses and heads beachside. Using canals, waterways, river and ocean he delivers gifts to children and seniors. This is a Florida Christmas Beachside.

Dit, Dot, Ditty, Dit, Dot a Ditty, Ditty

Nick Kaplan

It's nineteen sixty-one and we meet to celebrate with family and friends. Snow falling, booze flowing, faces glowing and laughter all round as Uncle Vinney tells a joke. Wonderland By Night is playing on the radio and Shu Bop takes over with Acapella renditions. Yo! Merry Christmas from Jersey City.

Most of All

Nick Kaplan

I am lost in the fifties tonight with tenor saxophones, Dion and the Belmonts, high hair, Chevvies and English leather. What can be better, what is to come? Love, heartache and memories. The rhythm of life, the music and the faces of those lost to history. I miss the snow.

First Christmas

Nick Kaplan

Pina Coladas flowing, wind and hurricane blowing, trees and lights glowing; it's Christmas in Florida. Treats and presents and people will stay as Santa comes and the elves do play. It's Christmas in Florida. The herons and gators sing praises of joy, as the pelican gulls and turtles chorus "Rejoice!"

Christmas Remembered

Nick Kaplan

Your attendance is voluntary; it may be the last time to visit the Grandparents. Colorful maple leaves are scattered on the new-fallen snow. They delight the eye; announcing winter. Relatives arrive bringing food, gifts, and stories to tell, while the brisk air and twilight chill evoke remembrances of past years.

Christmas Day

Nick Kaplan

Thirty minutes until gifts. I hope mine will be the big box; I was good this year. Fifteen minutes to go. Exultation mounting. Maybe it will be money, so I can buy it myself? Five minutes left. I'm so excited, I could explode in anticipation. Oh no, It's new underwear.

Christmas Poetry

We Brave Lads

Nick Kaplan

Christmas time and what we hear,
the hints, the praises, whispers in our ears.
Of bangles and baubles and gifts galore,
Of slippers, of dresses, of nighties, and more.
For our sweetie pie, our precious friend,
We shop and buy till dawn.
The package arrives in honest surprise;
Christmas day.

An Oldster's Christmas

Peggy Insula

No tree,
No Christmas lights
Are planned this Christmas.
Our kids are all grown;
The years have marched on.
We've grown too old to stress
Ourselves with all the holiday crush.
Simplicity, peace, contentment, and rest
Will fill our wooly stockings
And warm our hearts
Best for now.
Blessed Christmas!

Forgetful Mrs. Claus

Peggy Insula

"Yo! Santa!
Where you been?"
Mrs. Claus questions him.
"You been out all night!"
Open-mouthed, he turns to her.
"Why, Mrs. Claus, please do recall
It is the dawn of Christmas.
Lady, do you really think
In your most fantastic dreams
That tons of toys
Can deliver themselves
Without ME?"

Sensory Delights

Peggy Insula

Holiday holly,
Curly satin ribbons,
Wrapped packages piled high.
Carolers sing our favorite songs
As we sip creamy eggnog.
Scent of pine permeates the house
Along with aroma of sugar cookies.
Sincere toasts are cheerfully sipped;
Happy secrets are hastily whispered
As joy and excitement
Build, build, build!
It's Christmas!

Deadline

Peggy Insula

Elves scurry
Hither and yon
In Santa's busy workshop.
They're creating delightful, unique toys
Special-ordered by watchful children
Who prayerfully hope with starry eyes
That Santa has received their lists
And is willing to fulfill
Their deepest, greediest toy requests.
Christmas Day draws near.
Can the elves
Come through?

Santa At Work

Peggy Insula

Cookie crumbs
Dot Santa's beard
And sprinkle his coat
As, huffing, he stoops beneath
The tinsel-clad Christmas tree.
He delves into his bulging bag
For just the perfectly chosen gifts
To suit each family member.
Standing, he nods in satisfaction
With his wise choices.
He piles presents,
Then disappears.

Christmas Day Has Come

Kay Williamson

Tree lights blinking
Carolers are singing
Faces shining brightly in great anticipation
A day of joy and celebration
Children's laughter ringing out gaily
Presents opened ... faces beaming
A Christmas day filled with blessings
Day has ended now...all is quiet
Last embers dying in the fireplace
Christmas day has come

The Joy Of Giving

Linda Paul

I have no kids or grandkids to buy for
So I buy gifts for my great-nephews and
nieces
Who live very far away
And may not know me.
My sister, whose grandchildren these are
Sends me pictures of them with my gifts.
I almost cry when I see
Their delight.

The Reindeer Connection

Linda Paul

In the north up by Alaska
No presents could get through
So in 1899
The Post Office knew what to do.
They took a note from Santa
And recruited some reindeer
To take the mail deliveries
For Christmastime that year.
The creatures were so strong
They ate lichen on the way
The cold did not concern them
Just in time, they saved the day!
When the Gold Rush came along
The place was over-run
With new postal routes and offices
The reindeers' job was done.
They were adopted at a rescue
By a guy named Mr. Kringle
And they still make their deliveries
Their Christmas bells still jingle!

Short Stories and Memoirs

Christmas in Pennsylvania

Nick Kaplan

Heading west on Hwy 22, the vision of the passing countryside with shades of brown and dark green becomes dreary in the light rain.

Snow clouds start to form an ominous threat, while the occasional deer and buck dart in the distance. Faraway relatives arrive with gifts covered in splendid wrappings.

We meander to the dining room and, after exhaustive parlance, pray for the departed and absent. After dinner, the women talk on the porch while the men watch the game.

As snow falls and gifts are opened, we huddle near the fire for warmth and tales of Christmas past.

Holiday Hound

Nick Kaplan

Kozmo was his familiar name, but he was from the family of Quiescence Smooth Sailing. A great, great, great-grandson of Alexander of Synovia, known far and wide as the lazy Prince.

Kozmo, or Mo as he got older, was a lanky, brindle-colored Borzoi hound who stood up to my waist at two years old. Borzoi, now known as Russian wolfhounds, was once the favorite of aristocracy around the world due to their stamina at hunting wolves in the forest and on the Plaines of Russia. They were a passive bunch around humans and other dogs; they looked similar to Greyhounds with long hair.

Alas, the Bolsheviks wanted to expunge the existence of the monarchical symbols, so they sought out and slew twelve hundred dogs and puppies throughout the empire during their reign. The breed which survived was the gift dogs presented to monarchies and leaders around the world by Czar Nicholas before his demise.

Now Mo showed absolutely no signs of aristocracy except for lounging on the couch and chewing every little piece of kibble three or four times before swallowing. The Golden Retrievers in my family played rough and tore thru everything including plants and even a bush now and then in pursuit of the tennis ball.

Mo watched them and took notes on their behavior in play and schooling. On one occasion we hauled the entire clan of three retrievers and one Borzoi to a pond for swimming lessons and fun. Mo watched from the shore as the retrievers frolicked for tossed sticks, floating rubber-shaped bones, and other assorted training devices.

The fun they were having got the better of him and he leaped into the four-foot depth of water near the edge of the lake, splashing around with his stick-like legs to embrace the splendor of the cool, refreshing water. Borzois are fast creatures on land but in water, they resemble Nessie or the sea monster with slender long necks and a serpentine head breaking through the surface of the water. He couldn't deny it, he was having fun with the retrievers.

Now at Christmas time, we wrapped all the doggie treats in holiday wrap and planted them around the tree, and after a fun day making the (always up for anything) Goldens dig for the thrown tennis balls in the two-foot snow, we escorted them to the mudroom for towel rubs and hugs. Mo loved the hugs; however, Borzois have parallax vision when born and see items only two or three inches distant from their noses. They are called sighthounds and rely on a moving object rather than the smell of the prey. The snow-hidden toys did not interest him.

When it came time to release the hounds to their gifts from Santa in the formal sitting room, the Goldens would (like children) rush in and rip open bows, wrappings, and boxes. It was such a sight, paper flying everywhere and squeaky balls echoing a cacophonical sound throughout the house. Mo wined and fidgeted in a joyous rapture of the sight before him of all his retriever friends having fun.

After a short time, we would remove the gifts Santa had left and put the Goldens in their rooms. Returning, we bestowed on Kozmo his gift. It was a Wonder ball filled with squeaks, rattlers, noisemakers, and spaces for kibble to be hidden. Mo's eyes lit up when he rolled the three-inch ball, and it would make noise. When a piece of kibble exited the toy, he became ecstatic and pursued the ball, rolling it throughout the living room and beyond.

We finished our holiday cake and coffee and put Mo in his room (the laundry room) for an evening respite from the day's shenanigans. About two hours into this peace and quiet, my wife and I hear a clanking, and banging noise that would start and stop abruptly. I suggested we had a Ghost somewhere in the house, the wife proclaimed otherwise and began her investigation. Hi and lo we looked; could it be a tree branch outside tapping the frost-covered window during a gust of wind; no, we had no trees near the house. Maybe, Santa returned or, one of the Goldens brought in a stick from outside and is playing with it indoors; no, opening the door to their rooms displayed a pile of fur, snoring and exhausted from the day's events.

The laundry room was inspected, and Mo was just sitting on his faux fur extra-large doggie bed in the middle of the room. Our intrusion was surprising to the hound but, he showed no signs of standing, just a lazy head nod as a sign of indignity. Rodents, Racoons, and trapped birds or squirrels were ruled out after an exhaustive effort and search; however, just to be certain we bundled up and waited outside in the bitterly cold weather as the last effort to ferret out the elusive noise. Peering thru the laundry rooms' door window we finally solved the origin of the headache-producing sounds.

Mo had pushed the Christmas toy into the laundry room during play and was pushing it around, causing it to spin and make the creeks and clacking. After a few turns, he would push the toy under his faux-furred, extra-large doggie bed and pause to snooze. He so loved that toy and that Santa had come to visit him with his unique gift, that every Holiday since then he would wait for us, I mean Santa, to arrive bestowing his squeaky, clanky, rattlingly, headache machine which he would play with.

He would lick and roll around getting that last bit of kibble hidden inside for hours. Suffice it to be said, the Retrievers found the exercise playing with the toy exasperating and would walk away after a brief two-minute inspection.

They are all gone now, Mo and his Golden friends, but the memory of that first Christmas and how he loved that toy has stayed in my mind for many years. I am sure Santa is taking care of them at the North Pole. He was, no, maybe I should say they, were, my Holiday Hounds. Merry Christmas!!

When Rudolph Got His Chance

Dakota Williams

On the night before Christmas something happened to Rudolph. When Rudolph was at home sleeping, Rudolph's nose somehow turned orange. When Rudolph woke up, he saw that he had been sleeping on orange hay. But that's not all he noticed; he noticed his bright orange nose.

Rudolph went outside because he wanted to play antler tag and hide and go seek. But Rudolph was laughed out of all the reindeer games again. Rudolph ran away crying, as if the orange nose wasn't bad enough, now he couldn't play with the other reindeer. Rudolph kept crying and crying, "Why can't I play any games just because my nose is orange."

Just then Santa Claus saw Rudolph crying very, very hard. Santa asked Rudolph why he was crying and Rudolph said "Look, look at my nose. It changed, but that's not all, I got kicked out of the reindeer games again this year." Santa said, "I like you and your orange nose."

Rudolph stopped crying turned to Santa and said, "Really you mean that Santa!" Santa nodded patted Rudolph on the head and walked away.

Rudolph then began to prance away and run to his parents. Along the way Rudolph saw some bright red raspberries on a bush. Rudolph ran over to the berries and ate all the berries on the bush. Then slowly as he ran the rest of the way home his nose started turning red again.

Rudolph was so happy he did back flips in the air, and from that moment on Rudolph liked his nose no matter what color it was.

All She Wanted for Christmas

Richard McNamara

Growing up, Christmas was always a special time for me. I would plan my Christmas list months in advance and continue to revise until that special moment when I sent my letter to Santa. Of course, as with many people, some Christmases were better than others, but they were always a memorable time for me. As I started my family, I wanted to make my children's Christmas time as memorable as possible.

My oldest daughter was almost two when her second Christmas was approaching. We tried to get her in the spirit by reading her Christmas stories and watching shows and movies about the Yule season on TV. She would watch and listen to the characters in the shows, but she was still a little too young to grasp the whole concept, but we tried to instill in her that this was a special time of year.

She was attending daycare at a Baptist school in our town, and they, of course, had little plays and skits concerning the Christ child, and she participated as much as she could. But, like most children, she was drawn to the flashy toys and dolls in the TV commercials. She would sit with her grandfather in the afternoon after he had picked her up from daycare looking at the good old Sears catalog. Her Grandpa would ask her, "What about this cute doll? Do you like that one? How about a nice tricycle? Would you like one of those?"

Of course, the answer was usually yes. But then her grandpa noticed that she would also answer yes to almost everything he pointed out. As it got closer to Christmas, my wife and I, along with the grandparents, were always in a quandary as to what to buy her for Christmas.

I can remember going to the various department stores with her and roaming the aisles taking mental notes about the things she seemed to be interested in. Of course, the list was very long because everything to her was all shiny and sparkly and grabbed her eye as soon as she saw it. But she soon tired of it and moved on to the next eye-catcher. As time passed, we were getting more and more confused.

Her first Christmas was much easier. She was not quite a year old so buying a few small toys and something that she could push or pull and made noise made the whole shopping experience a lot less frustrating. Now she was almost two, and things were a lot harder. We wanted to get her nice things that she could play with and possibly some toys to help her learn her letters and numbers to help her as she grew. I didn't think it was going to be this hard! Did my parents go through the same issues with me?

While we enjoyed the feast of Thanksgiving with our family, our dilemma was only made more challenging as the various relatives would quiz our daughter about what she wanted for Christmas. As we listened in on the pretty much one-sided conversation, we realized that she didn't know what she wanted; she wanted everything! We were hoping to get some better ideas from her answers, but it was not to be. Later that evening, as we sat on the couch after putting her to bed, I said to my wife, "I think maybe we are trying too hard. Maybe the best idea is to get a few nice toys, maybe a tricycle and one of those See and Say toys and just see what happens. I mean, she is not yet two, and maybe we are expecting too much from her, plus the fact you know that our parents and some of the other relatives are going to get her things too."

She agreed, so we went to bed feeling a little more at ease about what to get to make her Christmas special.

That week, we picked out a Christmas tree for both our house and my parent's house. We had decided to actually open the gifts at my mom and dad's house, but we wanted a tree at home also. As we decorated the tree at home, you could see the look in our daughter's eyes as the tree was transformed from a bare green tree to a magical icon with many multicolored lights and sparkling ornaments twinkling in the dim living room in our house. She was proud of her involvement in the process as we would give her an ornament and help her find a nice spot on the tree for it to hang. It was almost tragic to see her expression of dismay as she accidentally dropped one of the fragile balls, and it shattered on the floor. We eased her mind and told her it was fine and that sometimes these things happen. She smiled again when I handed her another ornament to hang in the spot intended for the broken one.

When we were all finished, we sat on the couch and watched the light show from the twinkling lights and reflections from the shiny ornaments dance on the walls and ceiling of our living room. She was mesmerized by the beauty of the tree but seemed most fascinated with the icicles that were the last things to be put on. She carefully draped them across the limbs so that they hung down and lightly swayed with the small air currents wafting through the room.

When we went to my parent's house to help decorate their tree, she was the first to help because now she was an 'Old Hand' at decorating because she had decorated our tree at home. She and her mother and Grandmother toiled away stringing lights, hanging ornaments, and making the tree as pretty as ours at home. My dad and I made ourselves useful by staying out the way, untangling light strings, and opening ornament boxes. In short order, the tree was nearing completion. It was every bit as beautiful as the one at our house. My mother announced, "It's close to dinner time. I'll put the icicles on later."

Well, that wasn't going to happen. Our daughter insisted that they finish. She wanted to hang the icicles right away, so she could not only help, but she really liked the way they sparkled. My mother relented, and they finished the tree. Our daughter ate her dinner and went to sleep on the couch, watching the tree shimmering in the corner of the room.

The next few weeks were spent going to different stores buying presents, putting things on layaway, and wrapping gifts at night after she had gone to bed. We knew our parents were doing the same thing. My wife and I would often talk about what each of us had gotten the daughter and discuss what other things we might get her. I sat back and watched her wrap a small gift and thought about how my daughter might react as she opened it on Christmas Day. I had already bought a couple of things on my own for her and found things to buy for the wife, so I was feeling pretty good about the big day and really couldn't wait for the big day myself.

Not long before Christmas, we took our daughter to one of the larger department stores for her visit with Santa. We had taken her last year, but she was older now and would be more likely to remember it. As we stood in line, she looked around at the different displays and constantly talked about the things she saw. We asked her, "What are you going to ask Santa to get you for Christmas?"

Her answers were as varied as they had always been. She wanted this, and she wanted that. I had no idea what she was going to say when Santa asked her. Finally, it was her turn. We walked her up to where he was seated in an oversized, ornate chair surrounded by fake snow and tiny plastic reindeer attached to a little sleigh. As we got closer, I could see that this might not go so well. The closer we got, the tighter she held my hand. We got up to Santa, and he said,

"And who do we have here?"

"Melissa," I answered.

"Hi Melissa, would you like to sit on Santa's lap and tell him what you want for Christmas?"

All she did was shake her head no. Santa understood and said, "That's fine, Melissa. You can stand right there and tell me while you stand next to your parents."

It might have been fine for him, but it was definitely not fine for Melissa. For once, she was speechless. Santa handed her a lollipop and said, "That fine, Melissa. I'm sure Santa can find some nice things for you, and I still have to read your letter." He wished her a Merry Christmas, and we moved on. As we walked away, she kept looking back at Santa. I asked, "Do you want to go back and tell him what you want?" She shook her head, no. That weekend we helped her write her letter to Santa. She was OK with that. We put it in an envelope, addressed it to Santa Clause, North Pole, and put it in the mailbox the next morning.

The last few days before Christmas was a blur. We went to a little play at her daycare where all the little kids sang a couple of carols, showed their Christmas trees they had made by gluing bits of construction paper together, and had punch and cookies. We then went to Grandma's house, where there were a few presents under the tree already. Melissa was standing in the middle of the room, staring at the tree and presents, when Grandma said, "It won't be long now, honey. These are just a couple of gifts from me and your grandpa. Santa is going to bring the rest on Christmas Eve. Her eyes were bulging.

Christmas Eve was hectic, to say the least. We had to run all over town, picking up things on layaway at five different stores. Then we had to hurry home to wrap them while Melissa was at the grandparent's house. Once we had wrapped all the gifts, there was the matter of picking up things for Christmas dinner, shuttling the gifts to my parent's house, and putting them away until Christmas morning. Luckily my dad had taken Melissa to the zoo for the afternoon, so she wasn't at their house, so it was easy to move the gifts.

After dinner, Melissa went to sleep in her grandparent's bed, and we began bringing her gifts out of hiding and placing them under the tree. Some were wrapped, and others weren't. My father and I assembled a small kitchen set and put wheels on her new tricycle. Those also went next to the tree. After we finished, I carried Melissa to the car, and we went home to await the morning. I think I was more excited than Melissa was.

Christmas morning! Melissa was awake at the crack of dawn. We got dressed and jumped in the car for the quick trip to Grandma and Grandpa's house. We parked the car in the driveway, and she ran for the house. Once inside, she was awestruck by the sight of the presents under the tree. She went from one present to the other, touching them and tearing the wrapped packages open. My wife and I, as well as my parents, stood by watching with smiles on our faces as Melissa went from one present to the next opening, admiring, maybe even playing with something for a minute, then off to the next. Finally, she was done. As we opened our own presents, we were shocked as she walked past all of her new treasures and picked up a roll of masking tape from the coffee table. She then sat down in the middle of the living room and played with the tape for the rest of the morning!

Director of Operations
Earthly Manifestations Agency

First Staff Meeting
List of Attendees

Director of Operations – Miriam
Administrative Assistant – Manfred
Archivist – Benjamin

Charms & Amulets, Spells & Incantations, Potions & Brews Division - Hecate

Demigods and Minor Deities Division - Memnon

Enchanted Creatures Division – Elvis the Gerbil

Fairies, Nymphs, and Sprites Division - Alexis

Fairy Godpersons Division - Agatha

Gnomes and Trolls Division - Eragryph

Hauntings and Possessions Division – Green Zephyr

Honorable and Ancient Guardians Division –
Two Bears

Human Benefaction Division:
Scheduled   Disbursements   Section   -
Cranberry

Random Disbursements Section - Shellie

Intangibles Section - Thalia

Miscellaneous Magic and Mayhem Division
– Rosa Suarez

Myths, Fairy Tales, and Fables Division –
Little Red Riding Hood

Preternatural Manifestations Division -
Baobhan Sith

Wizards, Witches, and Warlocks Division –
Jefferson Baldwin

Director of Operations

Part One
First Day

Miriam carried another box of personal effects into her new office. It was more of a chore than she had anticipated. Not that she minded, of course; she was duly proud of her promotion, and it was well-deserved. But she felt more than a little intimidated, as if she had to prove herself worthy. After all, this was the first time a Muse had been appointed Director of Operations. She was in charge of the largest and most important department in the Earthly Manifestations Agency.

She gave a quick glance to the clock on the wall: 9:30. Her new secretary was due at eight o'clock. She caught herself getting annoyed, so she took a moment to relax and refocus. No need getting her blood pressure up on her first day.

She heard a commotion in the outer office, and she stuck her head out the door. A man in a tuxedo was arranging items on her secretary's desk.

"Excuse me," she said. "Who are you and why are you messing with things on my secretary's desk. Not that I have a secretary yet. Well, I do have a secretary, technically; I just haven't met her yet. But she should be here any minute. So, back to my original question. Actually, it was two questions, but I merged them into one, so I suppose it really was one question. Anyway, what was I asking?"

The man in the tux held up his hand and replied, "It's okay. I'm Manfred, your new administrative assistant. I'm sorry I'm late, but I was delayed in Entity Resources."

"I b-beg your pardon?" she stammered. "There must be some mistake. I requested a secretary from the Fairy Godmother Division."

"Yes; the division manager sent me, but it's called the Fairy Godperson section now. And I do prefer Administrative Assistant as a job title; I think it sounds so much more professional, don't you?"

"Well, sure, I, um, I suppose, um ... listen, if there's anything you need ...."

"No, ma'am, I have everything I need. Actually, I should be asking you that question. After all, I am your assistant."

"Hmmm, that's true. It's just, well, so weird for me. I've never had an assistant before. Okay, here's my first request: I want a staff meeting in the main conference room at one o'clock. I'd like all the division managers there, but since it's such short notice, deputies may attend in their stead, but only if absolutely necessary. I want them arranged around the table in alphabetical order by division name, plus you on my right and the archivist on my left. Can you take care of that for me?"

"I'd be delighted, ma'am. By the way, what is your name? I feel awkward calling you ma'am all the time."

"My name is Miriam."

"No, I mean your last name. I'm your assistant. I can't address you by your first name. You are a director now. It just isn't proper protocol."

"I'm sorry, Manfred, but Muses have only one name. You can call me Miriam or ma'am, your choice." She smiled, twirled around, and went back to her desk. She was already finding reasons to enjoy her new authority.

Manfred sat at his desk and sent a "Department – All Division Managers" email, announcing the mandatory staff meeting with the new Director. Then he leaned back in his chair and waited for the whines and complaints to start rolling in.

Part Two
Her First Staff Meeting

She opted to take her lunch in the first-floor cafeteria; she found the food there passably good, although she preferred to go to Dao Wu's Kosher Deli and Pizzeria around the corner. She made notes for the meeting on a yellow legal pad as she ate her plate of lizard lips and cricket hips, sautéed to a golden brown. Just before one o'clock, she took the transporter down to the second basement level and entered the conference room with no little trepidation. She had no idea what to expect, but she soon found out.

To describe the conference room at that particular moment in time as a scene of utter chaos would be a grand understatement. There were eighteen chairs neatly arranged around a long mahogany conference table, eight along each side and one at each end. Each place was identified with a name plate and a flag. Unfortunately, not a single attendee was sitting in a chair. Some were engrossed in animated conversations with their peers, others were hovering above the melee, one was shooting miniature globs of green goo at certain others, and two were actually hiding under the table.

Well, she thought to herself, it could be worse—no one had been killed or dismembered yet. She remained standing beside her seat at the near end of the table, held up her hands, palms outward, and gave forth a formidable blast of brain waves. The room immediately grew silent, and all faces turned toward her.

"Please take your seats," she instructed in a nice, even tone. She refused to show any outward signs of the annoyance that was welling up from deep within her.

"Manfred," she added, "would you get a towel for the Director of the Gnomes and Trolls Division, please? Thanks."

Manfred got up from his chair at her right hand and walked to the other end of the conference room. There, he opened a small closet door and took out a clean towel with the agency's emblem embroidered on it. On his way back, he gently handed it to a lawn gnome who was dripping with foul-smelling green slime. He then resumed his seat.

She continued, "Here's how this meeting will work. You all obviously know each other, but I don't know most of you, and most of you don't know me. I want each of you, in turn, to stand, introduce yourself, and give a brief—and I emphasize brief—overview of what your division does for the agency. We'll start with the Luck and Yuck group."

A grizzled old crone in a plain black witch's frock stood and pointed a crooked finger at Miriam. "You'll do well not to trifle with me, Muse. Luck and Yuck, indeed. You show us our proper respect or one morning you'll awaken as a toad."

"Don't even try to threaten me, Hecate. If I hadn't inspired the great Bard to write that "Double, double, toil and trouble; fire burn and caldron bubble" scene, you'd be nothing more than a footnote in a mythology textbook. Now, get on with your introduction as I instructed, or I'll make you a subordinate section of the Miscellaneous Division."

The witch hissed, but then thought better of escalating the confrontation. She pulled herself straight and tried to adopt a professional air, but her face looked more like someone had just made her eat a sour persimmon.

"I am Hecate, Manager of the Charms & Amulets, Spells & Incantations, Potions & Brews Division, known by some ne'er-do-wells as the Luck & Yuck group. We coordinate the correct and proper distribution and application of charms, spells, and potions throughout the world. Under the auspices of the Department Director, of course," she hastily added as she resumed her seat.

Next, a tall, handsome black man attired in fine, regal robes stood. "I am Memnon, Manager of the Demigods and Minor Deities Division. We provide secondary deific support for any agency operations, at the behest of the Director."

As the son of Eos sat down, the being on his left leapt from his chair onto the table. He was a grey gerbil, wearing what appeared to be a musketeer's uniform. "I am Elvis, no relation to the late human entertainer. I am Manager of the Enchanted Creatures Division. We provide clandestine support for agency operations at the request of the Director. On a personal note, I suspect the main qualification, for my title, is that I am able to sit in a chair." He bowed and sat down amidst much snickering.

After the rodent, a beautiful young woman, clad only in green leaves and vines, with flowers in her long brown hair, stood and said, "I am Alexis, Manager of the Fairies, Nymphs, and Sprites Division. I am a Dryad, or Wood Nymph. My group offers a variety of natural and supernatural services to any operation involving wooded areas or flowering fields. We have particular expertise in all phases of botany, including the apothecary properties of all known plants and trees."

The woman who followed looked like the archetypal grandmother. Her grey hair was pulled back in a bun. Gold-rimmed glasses rode low on her nose. Her gingham dress was undoubtedly hand-sewn. She had a gleam in her eye and a wand in her hand. "I am Agatha, Manager of the Fairy Godpersons Division. My personnel have their individual charges to serve, but when appropriate, we are all available, at a moment's notice, to perform low-level magic in support of any agency operation."

The lawn gnome, who had only partially succeeded in wiping away the green goo, stood in his chair to take his turn. "I am Eragryph, Manager of the Gnomes and Trolls Division. Our specialty is intelligence gathering and covert activities. Humans do not take us seriously, and we are able to use their erroneous assumption to our advantage."

He sat back down and continued to wipe away the green slime with the towel. As he did, a green cloudy vapor started to swirl above the adjacent seat. Gradually, a humanoid form began to take shape. The form spoke, and the temperature in the room dropped by several degrees.

"I am the Green Zephyr, Manager of the Hauntings and Possessions Division. We can possess the best and haunt the rest. We exist to serve." Then the greenish cloud dissipated.

The man in the next chair presented an impressive image. He wore a headband with several feathers, and he had several lines of different colors painted across each side of his face. He wore a buckskin jacket, pants, and moccasins. He stood up and said, "I am Two Bears, Manager of the Honorable and Ancient Guardians Division. We provide protection for agency personnel while on assignment, and also for designated innocents. We seldom lose a charge, and then only if the opposing magic is very strong."

When the ancient Plains warrior sat down, three diminutive young ladies stood simultaneously. The first one said, "I'm

Cranberry. I'm a North Pole Elf. I represent the Scheduled Disbursements Section." The second one said, "I'm Shellie. I'm a tooth Fairy. I represent the Random Disbursements Section." The third one said, "I'm Thalia. I'm a Muse. I represent the Intangibles Section."

Cranberry spoke again," We represent the three sections of the Human Benefaction Division. We don't do battle; we award and reward, based on the yearly calendar, specific behavior, or special needs." Then all three sat back down.

A little girl then stood. She wore a red cloak. She said, "I'm Little Red Riding Hood. I represent the Myths, Fairy Tales, and Fables Division. And don't get any wrong ideas; I'm more than four hundred years old. Our function is to make sure that every time a story is played out, it remains faithful to the original."

The woman whose turn it was next was the palest entity in the room, even counting the cloud of vapor. She was dressed in black, but her cloak couldn't hide her fire red hair. She spoke with a hint of a Scottish brogue.

"I am Baobhan Sith. I am a Highland Vampire. I am Manager of the Preternatural Manifestations Division. We provide the agency with vampires, werewolves, the occasional mummy, whatever is needed to accomplish the mission."

"I am Jefferson Baldwin," the next person said. "I am actually a sorcerer, just to keep the record straight. I am Manager of the Wizards, Witches, and Warlocks Division. We are available at all times for on-site magical intervention."

The final representative stood and introduced herself. "I am Rosa. I am the daughter of Carmen Suarez and Kokopelli. I am the Manager of the Miscellaneous Magic and Mayhem Division. We provide creative approaches when the agency decides to color outside the box."

Miriam stood up again. "Thank you for keeping the introductions brief. Now, I'm sure you have plenty of questions for me, but I'm afraid you will have to hold onto them until later. I will not be answering any questions at this meeting. That is not the reason we are here. Besides wanting to meet each of you my first day on the job, there are two very important things I want to tell you. These two things may dispel some of your questions and/or concerns. However, before I get to them, I have a question for the representatives from the three sections of the Human Benefaction Division. I appreciate the three of you being here, but where is your manager? Why isn't he here himself, rather than sending his three section chiefs?"

The ensuing silence was deafening. An undercurrent of murmurs made a unsettling sensory backdrop for the stricken looks on many of the faces. Nobody showed any sign of willingness to answer her questions.

"Thalia, you're a fellow Muse. Surely you will give me a straight and honest answer. Where is your boss, and why isn't he or she here?"

Thalia winced, as if she had been jabbed with a sharp stick. She looked back and forth to Cranberry and Shellie, but they were carefully avoiding her visual pleas for help.

"Okay, I want an answer, and I want it now!"

Miriam was quickly running out of patience. The archivist leaned toward her and whispered, "I'm not sure why they are so hesitant to tell you, Miriam, but the Manager of the Human Benefaction Division is Saint Nicholas."

"Santa Claus?" she blurted. They all released their breath through their clenched teeth, creating a sound like someone opening a giant bottle of a carbonated beverage. "You're telling me that Saint Nick is the Manager of Human Benefaction? I'm a Muse; I worked with Thalia, yet I never knew who the manager was. This is amazing."

She leaned over to the archivist and asked, "Am I the only one in the room who didn't know?" He nodded. She sighed.

"Well, now that the big secret is out, perhaps we can get back to business. As I said, there are two things I want you to know right up front. First, I know that all too often, a new boss starts making changes right away just to assert her authority. I want you to know I won't be doing that. Certainly, I will make changes as they are needed, but only after careful consideration and consultation.

"Second, as you all are no doubt aware, I am the first Muse to be appointed to this post. The significance of my selection is not lost on me. In my heart, I know that the leadership of this agency put me here with my particular talents clearly in mind. I want all of you to start thinking about how I can benefit your divisions with my special abilities, and how together we can enhance the gains humans derive from our services.

"Okay, that's all I have for you right now. Please, hold all your questions and comments for our next meeting, which, I promise, will have a longer lead time. And if you have something to ask me or tell me that in your opinion just cannot wait, please submit it to me via email. I promise I will read and give proper consideration to everyone."

Part Three
Sorting Through the Gripes

With her two assistants in tow, she headed to her office. Rather than sit behind her desk and lord over them, she chose to have the three of them sit at a small, square table on the other side of her office. Manfred automatically sat on her right, and the archivist, Benjamin, took a seat on her left. Benjamin was a Scrivener Elf, and she had thoughtfully arranged to have a booster seat installed in that chair for his benefit.

"Okay," she said, "let's give them about fifteen minutes to get back to their offices and fire off their first emails. My philosophy is, if they're not griping, they're not happy. As long as we get a nice big stack of emails, we can be sure everything is okay. It's when we don't hear from them that we can start worrying. In the meantime, I have a few things to discuss among the three of us.

"Number one, I want you to know that I am going to be leaning on the both of you rather heavily for a while, until I get to know my way around the job. As a Muse, I spent most of my time out there, inspiring my charges, and very little time here at the agency headquarters. It's going to be up to you to make sure I don't step on the wrong toes or listen to the wrong advice. And always remember, what is said in here, stays in here. I will be telling you things that should not even be whispered outside this office. Also, I expect you to be open and candid with me during these discussions. Please be respectful, but truthful.

Two, I'm going to be making some major changes to the internal structure of the department. Some of the changes will not be received well. I'm going to rely on you guys to run interference for me—head off any direct attacks and put a happy face on all my decisions.

Third and finally, I don't deal in gossip. I don't want you discussing inappropriate subjects with friends and peers outside this office, and I don't want you coming to me with unsubstantiated rumors, no matter how juicy. Let's stick to the facts, always."

The two nodded their agreement. They were starting to like their new boss.

"Manfred, go ahead and check the emails. We should have quite a few by now. Print them, assemble them by division, and we'll start working through them in, say, fifteen minutes. Benjamin, check the archives for everything you can find on Saint Nick as a division manager. I want to know who appointed him, and when, and if there are any strings attached. See you both back here in a quarter of an hour."

When they left, she went around and sat down in the brand-new executive chair behind her desk. She took off her glasses and rubbed the bridge of her nose. The job wasn't anything like she had thought it would be, but that was almost universally true. She was sure, however, that she was up to the task. In fact, she already could feel the anxiety giving way to excitement. The first thing she needed to do was replace that fat man in the red suit.

She was pleased to see both her assistants return in only ten minutes. The three of them resumed their places at the table.

"Before we tackle that impressive stack of emails," she began, "I want the info on Saint Nick." She looked straight at Benjamin.

"Well," he said, and then cleared his throat, "it seems our right jolly old elf has been in his management position for a little more than two hundred years. From what I can determine, based on a very thorough search of the records, he never was formally appointed. I can only surmise that since he is, without a doubt, the most well-known member of our agency, worldwide, he was automatically put in charge of the Human Benefaction Division."

"Thank you, Benjamin. Unfortunately, I suspected as much. I'm going to share my first confidence with you two: I despise the practice of honorary appointments for figureheads. I'm willing to bet a bumblebee's butt the fat man has never attended a staff meeting. Don't misunderstand—I have nothing against Santa Claus. I think he's doing a wonderful job, and there's the rub. He's much too busy, as well as too important, to attend regular meetings, but I can't afford any absentee managers. I'm here to revitalize the department, not to babysit prima donnas. I'm going to have to replace him as manager, and the sooner the better.

"Manfred, I want you to draft two or three different letters to Santa, letting him down gently. Glorify his job performance and reputation; make it sound as if we're doing him a favor. Benjamin, search the records for some potential replacements. I want someone who can lead the division, and, just as importantly, someone who has the time to devote to the job. It's the largest division we have, with the biggest slice of the budget. We need to make sure the agency is getting its money's worth."

"Forgive my directness," Benjamin ventured, "but you said we should feel free to candidly express ourselves within the confines of your office." Miriam nodded her assent. "Is there a personal agenda behind the removal of Santa as the manager of his division? It will certainly appear so to the agency as a whole."

"You voice a valid concern, Benjamin, and I suspect your assumption will prove correct. The simple answer is 'No.' I will admit to being mildly annoyed that one of my division managers was not present at my first staff meeting, but my personal feelings will never affect a decision of this magnitude. Santa must be replaced because, simply said, he is too important to be saddled with the additional responsibility. My dilemma is who to select as the appropriate replacement. I do have someone in mind, but as I said, if either of you has any suggestions, please let me know."

She turned to Manfred and noted that he had a significant stack of emails in front of him, even more than she had anticipated. "Did we hear from everyone?" she asked.

"All but Baobhan Sith in the Preternatural Manifestations Division," he answered.

"Hmmmm," she voiced with an undertone they didn't quite understand. "Okay, let's dig in, then. Let me hear the ones from the Human Benefaction Division first; might as well get it over with. First, let me ask … are there any from Saint Nick himself?"

"No, nothing from him or any of his executive assistants, but there are plenty from his three division managers."

She sighed. "Go ahead, let's get those done first."

"Yes, ma'am, er, excuse me, yes, Miriam," he began. "We have three from Cranberry in the Scheduled Disbursements Section: one regarding a request from the Easter Bunny for an increase in his annual budget due to the skyrocketing cost of chocolate; one addressing a request from Punxatawney Phil, which was forwarded from his boss in the Enchanted Creatures Division, pleading that he be reassigned to the Scheduled Disbursements Section [Cranberry recommends disapproval, by the way]; and another one from Cranberry, recommending that the budget for the Lucky Penny Group be reduced by fifty percent, with the excess released for other needs ... at her discretion, of course."

"You see? It's starting already. The Human Benefaction Division wields too much power, and it controls an excessive portion of our annual budget. Everyone wants a piece of the pie, as it were. Even those within the division feel slighted if they aren't a part of the Scheduled Disbursements Section. We must devise a way of making everyone within the entire department feel equally important to the organization. What do the other two sections have to say?"

"Well, we have only one from Shellie, recommending that a request from the Tooth Fairie for transfer to the Scheduled

Disbursements Section be disapproved. Thalia blessed us with a three-page prattle which, if I get the gist correctly, suggests that rabbits' feet be removed from the official list of recognized talismans."

"Bless her heart. Thalia is the only one to send a truly altruistic request. Everyone else is just jockeying for position in the great race for more cash or more power." Miriam sighed again. "Okay, here's what we'll do. Manfred, belay my order to draft a letter to Santa. I'll call him myself, this afternoon. If he's too busy to take my call, he can just get the bad news from his answering machine.

"In the meantime, prepare an email response to Cranberry. Tell her that the request for a budget increase from the Easter Bunny will get sent upstairs with my strong recommendation for approval, the Groundhog will remain with the Enchanted Creatures Division [info Elvis on that, he needs to know what that rodent is up to, if he doesn't already], and the Lucky Penny Group will be transferred to the Random Disbursements Division with a 100% increase in budget and staff."

"Okay, I understand moving the Lucky Pennies to Unscheduled, in fact I agree, but why double their budget?" Benjamin asked.

"Lucky pennies come from two sources," Miriam explained. "Most of them are placed by our group, but some are actually lost by humans. Now, as we all know, in order to bring good luck, a penny must be found face up. Obviously, all the pennies placed by our people are that way, but those dropped by humans have a fifty-fifty chance of landing face down, and that is bad luck. I want the Lucky Penny Group to take on the additional responsibility of tracking down these randomly misplaced pennies and turning them lucky side up."

"Wow, that could be time consuming," Manfred commented.

"Hence the doubling of their budget and staff. Okay then, let's move on to the Random Disbursements Section. Let's send Shellie an email concurring with her recommendation that the Tooth Fairy's request for transfer be disapproved. There's no way he falls within the definition of scheduled disbursements. He just wants to get in with the big players. Well, he's going to get what he wants, but not in the way he envisioned. But I digress. Tell Thalia I will send her recommendation regarding the rabbits' feet to the boss with my strongest recommendation for approval. Yuck! I can't believe people are still so barbaric these days!"

They worked on through the afternoon, addressing the questions and concerns of most of the division managers, some legitimate and some petty, until a deep growl from Miriam's stomach announced it was well past suppertime. They adjourned for one hour, agreeing to return to finish the emails before calling it a night.

Miriam made a quick run to Dao Wu's for a corned beef on rye and a pickle, which she brought back to her office to eat. As she sat at the table, greedily chomping away at her sandwich, she suddenly got the feeling she was not alone. She slowly and carefully scanned the room. There, in the far corner, behind the Ficus tree, was a dark but unmistakable human shape.

"Hello, Baobhan. Nice of you to join me this evening," Miriam said.

"Good eve, my dear. Would you be offerin' a poor soul a slice of that pickle?"

"I didn't know Highland Vampires had a taste for kosher dills." Miriam motioned for her guest to have a seat across from her at the table.

"Aye, it's a particular guilty pleasure of mine," the vampire admitted. Her fiery red hair contrasted strikingly against her black cape, even under the pale fluorescent lights in the office ceiling.

"Then please, help yourself," Miriam replied. "I was hoping you'd show up this evening, since you're the only division manager who didn't submit any whiny emails."

"As you know full well, whining is not my style. You can always count on me to voice my concerns directly, in person whenever possible."

"I thank you for that, Baobhan. I hope I can count on your support for my efforts to maximize the efficiency of this department, too, now that I'm in charge."

"Aye, that you can. I and my entire staff congratulate you on your well-deserved, albeit most unexpected, promotion. You have been most helpful to us."

"When I first proposed that I give special attention to your group, I was ridiculed by friend and foe, but the success of the recent plethora of vampire books and movies has silenced even my most die-hard critics. And I must admit, working closely with some of your members was delightfully enlightening for me as a Muse. I shall miss that."

"I'm sure Thalia shall provide an adequate replacement, although I am certain we'll not see one of your caliber again."

Miriam bowed her head respectfully. "I'm flattered."

"May I tell you something, woman to woman, as it were?" the Sith asked, suddenly changing the subject.

"Of course, my dear," Miriam replied, glad her evening visitor finally got to the point of her visit.

"Beware. There is a dangerous plot afoot. I know not from whom, but I can feel it. You would do well to see about doubling the security in this building."

"I thank you for that, Baobhan. I respect your intuition in such matters. I will do as you recommend."

"You will make a fine director, indeed. The agency is lucky to be having you. And now, my dear friend, I must go. Nighttime is my busy time, as you know." Baobhan waved and faded away.

Not two minutes later, Benjamin and Manfred walked in, laughing over a joke one of them had shared in the hallway. As they entered, their grins disappeared.

"Wow, it's freezing in here. Who turned up the air conditioning?"

"Oh, I hadn't noticed," Miriam replied, and she really hadn't.

Part Four
The Law of Unforeseen Consequences

It took them a little more than an hour to work off the remaining stack of emails. Rosa wanted a more clearly defined mission statement for her division. She felt her people were not being used to their full abilities and morale was suffering. Baldwin complained most vehemently that his division was getting less and less support from Hecate's "Luck & Yuck" operation; he pointed out, using specific examples, that his division's effectiveness and timeliness were suffering as a direct result of her eroding cooperation.

"Okay, it's time to make a few of those changes I mentioned at the meeting. I know it's a bit soon, but things are even worse than I anticipated. Here's what I want; you two put out the appropriate official notifications and documents.

"Effective immediately, the Luck & Yuck division becomes a part of the 3W division. Hecate is relieved as Manager, pending recommendations by a review board, which will be convened as soon as practical. Also, effective immediately, the Fairy Godpersons Division becomes a part of the Honorable and Ancient Guardians Division. Agatha is to be relieved as Manager, but gently; she has not done anything wrong, and I will personally reassign her as soon as I can sit down with her, and we can talk about her goals and aspirations.

"Lastly, I want Rosa's under-utilized division renamed the Unforeseen Consequences Division. Every action, human and supernatural, has at least one unintended reaction. I want her personnel trained to handle anything that may come up. It's a big order, but I think she's up to the challenge. She's right; her division is not being used to its full potential. This should solve that problem."

"But that leaves only eleven divisions," Manfred said, sounding horrified. "We've always had thirteen divisions. Thirteen is the prime lucky number in our realm."

"Yes, I'm aware of that, but eleven is a powerful number, too. It is the ultimate, perfect number in numerology. In any event, we can't let superstition dictate the structure of our organization."

Miriam stood up, saying, "Okay, you two, take care of the paperwork for the changes I mentioned and then go home. I have a phone call to make."

Her two assistants bid her a good night and left, while she went back to her desk to call the North Pole. She opened her center desk drawer and took out a small notebook. She turned to the page that listed all the private personal numbers within the department. Pausing a moment to organize her thoughts, she then dialed Santa's number. As she suspected, she got a recorded message. At the tone, she spoke clearly and carefully into the phone.

"Hello, Santa. This is Miriam, the new Director of Operations. I'm calling to let you know I'm relieving you as Manager of the Human Benefaction Division. This is not the result of any wrongdoing on your part. You are just too busy and important to carry that responsibility. It's not fair to you or the division. I will make the official announcement tomorrow that the Tooth

Fairy is assuming control of the division. We should talk more about this, but I would rather do it face to face. Let me know what your schedule will allow. Good night."

As she hung up the phone, Manfred stuck his head through the doorway and said they had finished the requisite paperwork and were headed home. Miriam sat back and sighed. It had been a long and emotionally draining first day, but she felt satisfied that she had accomplished some good things for the organization.

Just then, a terrible ruckus arose from the hallway outside her office. A series of loud popping sounds were followed by yells and screams. Overcome by curiosity, she walked to her door and out through the outer office. She opened the door to the hallway and froze. There, on the floor, right in front of her outer office door, were Manfred and Benjamin. Each was deathly still, with several bright red stains on his clothing, and what appeared to be a pool of blood expanding on the hallway carpet.

And what was that smell? Nutmeg? More popping sounds came from the far end of the hall, and a bullet ricocheted off the door frame just inches from her head. She yelped and ducked back behind the door, slammed it shut, and threw the safety bolt. She crouched down against the wall, trying very hard to control her breathing so she wouldn't hyperventilate and pass out.

In the midst of all the commotion, her desk phone began to ring. She was tempted not to answer it, but her curiosity, as well as a bit of intuition, got the better of her. On all fours, she crawled around behind her desk, reached up, and grabbed the phone. She answered tersely.

"This had better be important," she snipped.

"I believe it is," the voice on the other said without hesitation. "I'm calling from the North Pole. Cranberry has launched a coup d'état. Santa is dead, and now she's planning to move against your headquarters. She has several dozen well-armed elves with her, and she means business."

"I didn't know about Santa. I'm so sorry. But Cranberry is already here. Her troops have started the attack already. I'm barricaded in my office. My two assistants are dead. Tell me, who are you and why are you risking this call?"

"My name is Krystall. I'm an Engineer Elf in Product Development. I want you to know that the coup is not widely supported. At least a dozen elves loyal to Santa were killed during the initial assault. Some of Cranberry's insurgent elves manufactured grenade launchers and AK-47s during off-duty hours. None of us suspected a thing."

"Okay, Krystall, I want you to listen very carefully. I'm declaring a state of martial law at the North Pole, and I'm putting you in charge. You have temporary authority over everyone and everything there. Keep me advised as often as you can. We need to put a lid on this as swiftly as possible. You take care of your place, and I'll take care of mine. Good luck to both of us." Then the line went dead. And then the lights went out.

"Well," Miriam said to herself, "I guess I'll have to do this the old-fashioned way." She lit a candle, sat cross-legged under her desk, and concentrated.

Part Five
Helles und Dunkles

Rosa was sitting next to a small fire, meditating. She was alone. The smell of nutmeg filled the air inside her humble adobe pueblo. She often used spices to enhance her concentration. She lived in an ancient cliff-dwelling community in New Mexico, in the same manner as did her ancestors for many generations.

"Rosa. Rosa, can you hear me? It's Miriam." The voice seemed to come from the smoke of the fire.

"Yes, Miriam, I can hear you," Rosa answered, keeping her eyes closed.

"Cranberry has taken control of the North Pole. Santa is dead. Now she and her renegades are attacking the agency. My two assistants are dead. We're all in grave danger."

"Yes, Miriam, I foresaw these things. I momentarily teleported to help Manfred and Benjamin make the transition to the next life. This afternoon, after the meeting, I asked Baobhan Sith to visit you with a warning of the impending danger. It is important for you to know that we are all standing by to render assistance.

"There is one matter of which you are probably unaware. Cranberry and her rebels are being assisted by Hecate. They have spells and potions, so it will take strong medicine to defeat them.

"Two Bears himself is working as we speak to establish a protective barrier around you, and Elvis is summoning some fearsome creatures to assist in the defense of the agency. Together, we shall subdue these cowardly traitors."

Miriam was so overcome by the show of dedication and support, she felt tears streaming down her cheeks. "Thank you, Rosa," was all she was able to say.

As the psychic contact with Rosa evaporated, Miriam reached into another desk drawer and took out a small glass vial with a natural cork stopper. She uncorked the vial and put it against her cheek, capturing several teardrops. Tears shed from joy or gratitude contained powerful magic, and she thought she knew exactly how she would use these.

More explosions, stronger and closer this time, rocked the room, and bullets once again bounced along the hallway walls. Suddenly a loud ka-boom blasted her office door off its hinges. Acrid smoke billowed into the room. As the haze cleared, Miriam saw Cranberry, dressed in camouflage fatigues and holding a grenade launcher, surrounded by several other elves, similarly dressed, and pointing automatic rifles in her general direction.

"Hello, Cranberry. I've been expecting you."

"Yes, it's hard to keep a secret around here. No matter. You no doubt know why we're here. We can do this the easy way, or we can do this the hard way. Please tell me you choose the hard way. I'd like nothing better than to blow your cowardly creative carcass to kingdom come."

"Yes," Miriam thought to herself. "It's working. She's already becoming alliterative. She's ready for the final push."

Aloud, she said to Cranberry, "As you wish, my dear. You may give me your best shot."

"Alright, my fine fellow freedom fighters, fire!" she yelled to her troops. They opened up with their AK-47s switched to fully automatic. Several dozen bullets hurtled towards Miriam and then came to an abrupt halt just a foot from her body. They hovered momentarily, and then started seeking other entryways, probing all around the invisible protective barrier surrounding Miriam as she stood there.

She stood there, nonplussed, and concentrated as she never had before. "Cranberry, my dear," she thought, "I have seldom met a more powerful life force. You are truly a great leader as well as a fierce warrior. The world will sing your praises, but only if your story gets told properly. And who better to tell of your exploits than you yourself. You must, for the sake of future generations, write a book of your wondrous victory here today."

Cranberry at first looked confused, then pleased, and finally determined. She took two steps forward, totally distracted from the task at hand. Her hand-picked comrades in arms turned their collective gaze upon her. At that second, a pack of growling grey wolves, led by a huge brown wolf-like creature, rushed through the open doorway. The werewolf threw Cranberry to the floor, pinning her with his large paws armed with razor-sharp claws. The wolves pounced on the distracted rebels, two per elf. The carnage was so ghastly and grisly, Miriam had to turn away.

When she looked again, there was blood and bits of elf everywhere—floor, walls, and even the ceiling. Cranberry remained pinned to the floor, unable to move. The werewolf was growling, menacingly, and drool dripped from his gaping jaws onto her terrified face, but he made no move to finish her off.

Miriam stepped out of her protective shell, and the buzzing bullets fell to the floor. She walked over to Cranberry, held out the vial of tears she had so recently collected, and poured the contents onto Cranberry's forehead. For a brief moment, a glow encompassed the elf's head, and then she passed out.

The werewolf stepped away from the unconscious elf and looked directly at Miriam, as if awaiting further instructions.

"I thank you, sir. Without the timely coordination between you and Elvis' wolves, we surely would have perished in a most unpleasant way. Please convey my sincere regards to Baobhan Sith."

He bowed briefly and then walked out of the room. There was a spring and a swagger in his step. The pack of grey wolves followed him.

Miriam knelt beside Cranberry and cradled her head in her lap. She stroked the elf's hair and face until she opened her eyes.

"Hello, Cranberry, my dear. How do you feel?"

"My head hurts," she replied.

"I should imagine it does. Do you remember what happened?" she asked.

"I do, but everything echoes in my head, as if it were a story told to me by someone else."

"Yes, you were not yourself, my dear. You were under the spell of Hecate."

"That wicked old crone! I hope she gets what she deserves. Poor Santa!" Cranberry began to cry.

"That's right, my dear. Let it all out. I assure you; I will deal with Hecate most harshly. Tomorrow we will make all this right."

"Oh, Miriam, you really are a wonderful director," Cranberry said, trying to smile through her grief. "It's very odd, though. I have the strangest feeling I need to write a book about all this. Weird, huh?"

"Well, I believe that can wait, my dear, but no, it's not all that weird."

Part Six
And So It Goes

Cranberry returned to the North Pole the following morning, fully recovered from her harrowing experience. Overnight, Krystall had secured the arctic outpost, and everything was running smoothly. As it turned out, the engineer elf had no ambition to hold onto her emergency leadership appointment permanently; she was glad she was able to assist the new director, but she was anxious to get back to the Product Development Lab. Cranberry humbly accepted her reappointment as the leader of the Scheduled Disbursements Section, and she enjoyed working with her new boss, the Tooth Fairy, who managed the Human Benefaction Division effectively and always within budget.

Miriam was relieved to learn there was already a procedure in place to acquire a new Santa Claus, although she was a bit incensed that females were excluded. Specific male elves were designated as 'Santas in Training,' and when a vacancy occurred, which happened more often than she would have guessed, the senior designee spontaneously evolved into the next Saint Nick. She didn't get all the details, nor did she want them, but she was glad the children would not have to forego their presents under the tree because of a hexed elf.

Meritorious Service Awards were presented to Baobhan Sith, Two Bears, Elvis the Gerbil, and Rosa Suarez in a special ceremony held to honor their invaluable assistance. Benjamin and Manfred were immortalized with large portraitures hung in the agency's main lobby. Hecate was stripped of her powers and exiled to Kokomo Key, Florida, where she had to earn a living selling souvenirs to obnoxious tourists. Miriam changed her mind about combining the 3W and the Luck & Yuck divisions, and she appointed Albus Dumbledore as the new Manager of the Charms & Amulets, Spells & Incantations, Potions & Brews Division, with the provision that he would be excused temporarily whenever he was needed for a new Harry Potter movie.

In her spare time, Cranberry wrote a book about the North Pole Insurrection, as she called it. She had never thought about writing a book before the incident, but it was almost as if she couldn't avoid writing it. To her credit, the account was accurate as well as spellbinding. It made the national bestseller list in the fiction category. After all, what did humans know about the supernatural world, anyway?

Kids!

Richard McNamara

The week after Thanksgiving is tough. After a couple of days off for the holiday, going back to work is rough. I park the bike in the carport and slog into the house like I've been working for days. I toss my helmet, gloves, and jacket on top of the workbench in the utility room and make a beeline for my recliner. Once I am completely comfortable, I yell out, "Make me a tea," to which the wife replies, "Make your own tea. I'm cooking dinner."

"Where are the girls? Maybe one of them can make me a tea," I said, knowing my request would fall on deaf ears.

"You won't get anything out of them," my wife Judy replied. "They're pouring over the Sears toy catalog. You won't see them for hours. Whatever you do, don't ask them what they want for Christmas."

I sat in my chair, hoping someone would feel sorry for me and bring me a tea, but after a few minutes, it became perfectly clear that I was on my own and that if I wanted tea, I would have to get it myself. With much groaning and grumbling, I got up and stumbled into the kitchen. "Couldn't find anyone to wait on ya, huh," the wife said as I poured tea from the pitcher.

Not wanting to start world war three, I put the pitcher back in the fridge and carried the glass of tea back to my recliner, grumbling all the way. As I sat back down, Judy said, "What did you say?"

"Nothing, dear."

"I didn't think so," she said with a chuckle in her voice.

I watched TV as I slowly drank my tea. It wasn't long until I was sound asleep, as usual. It was a short-lived nap because pretty soon, my oldest daughter Melissa was shaking my shoulder, "Dad. Dad. Wake up. It's time to eat." Slowly I sat my chair upright and tried to stand. The first couple of tries didn't work out so well, but on the third try, I managed to stand almost upright. Melissa took my glass from me and ran to the kitchen to fill it up again. I made it to the table just as

Judy sat the meatloaf down in the middle of the table.

As usual, dinner was great. I was almost feeling human again when I made the mistake of asking Melissa and her sister Christie, " Well. Did you find anything in the toy catalog you might want for Christmas?" Judy just shook her head, got up from the table, and walked into the kitchen. As she walked away, she mumbled, "Just remember. You asked for it."

Both of them talked at once as they ran to Melissa's bedroom. I had just sat down in my recliner when they ran back down the hall. Melissa dumped the catalog in my lap while Christie had a notepad with quite a few pages folded over and written on in three different colors of ink. They both started flipping the pages of the catalog as it lay on my lap. Since they were so excited and were talking over each other, I had no idea what they were saying. "Whoa," I said. "Let's try this one at a time."

Christie, who was just over four years old, blurted out, "I want a bike, and a See and Say, and a kitchen." Then Melissa took over.

"I want skates, and a pogo stick, and a bike." It was then that Christie handed me the notepad. "There's a lot more things on this list than what you two just said. So what do you really want?"

"Okay, Dad," Melissa said, taking the notepad away from me and flipping through several pages. We want everything from page 234 to page 486 in the catalog. At that, they grabbed the book and went into Melissa's bedroom.

As they walked down the hall, I let out a feeble, "Hey. You know that's a lot of stuff." "We know, Dad. But we know you can get it for us," she said as they disappeared into her room.

Judy came out of the kitchen and patted me on the head, "I tried to warn you."

The following week or so was terrible. Every night when I got home, it was the same thing. After dinner, the girls would drag out that catalog and, with the book on my lap, would flip through page after page of new stuff they had found. It got so that I didn't want to come home. Then one night, I shut the bike off down the street and coasted up the driveway so they wouldn't know I was home. I snuck in the utility room door and tried not to let them hear me when Judy said, "What are you doing?"

"Shhh. I don't want the girls to hear me."
"It's okay. I had a long talk with them today, and they have a new plan now."

"What are they gonna do, rob Sears," I said with fear in my eyes.

"No, stupid. They're gonna ask Santa. So you're off the hook. They're in there right now, making up their lists. Well. Melissa is doing both lists because Christie can't write."

About a week later, I came home with a bit of spring in my step and a twinkle in my eye. The wife noticed the difference in my demeanor and asked, "What are you up to?"

"Never you mind. It's a secret," I said with a big smile on my face.

"I hope it's not one of your crazy ideas," she said, glaring over her shoulder as she went down the hall.

After dinner, we all were in the living room watching TV. It was dark out, and it was about a quarter till seven. I got up and opened the living room curtains. "What are you doing?" Judy asked.

"I just wanted to be able to see outside," I said. "Can't we open the curtains once in a while?"

She gave me 'the look' as she went back to her magazine. At seven o'clock, I saw a bearded face at the corner window. Melissa saw it too. "Dad! There's someone at the window," she yelled.

Sitting up in my chair, I said, "Where." I didn't see anything, just as the face appeared again.

"There," she said, pointing to the window.

It was then that Santa Clause walked to the front door and sang out in his booming voice,

"Are Christie and Melissa here?"

Both of the girls stood there frozen with their mouths hanging open. I finally said to them, "You gonna let him in?"

When he knocked again, Melissa got up and opened the door. He entered the room with a loud 'Ho, Ho, Ho.' Sitting down on the couch, he beckoned to Melissa to sit on his knee. It took a minute for her to respond, but once she was seated, Santa said, "And what can I bring you for Christmas, dear?"

"I want a desk so I can do my schoolwork," Melissa said.

"Don't you want anything else?" Santa asked.

"Yeah, but I can't think of them right now."

"Okay, dear. I'll see what I can do. Now, you jump down, and remember, I'm always watching."

Christie wasn't having any part of Santa, so Judy walked her over to where he was seated. She wouldn't sit on his knee, so she just stood beside him. "So, Christie. What can I bring you for Christmas?"

She looked at him, then her mother, and then at me. "Tell Santa what you want, baby. That's why he's here," I said trying to encourage her.

With her voice cracking, she finally said, "I want a kitchen just like mommy's." As soon as she said that, she ran over to Judy and stood next to her, looking at Santa.

Santa got up from the sofa and, with a final 'Ho, Ho, Ho,' went out the door and into the night. The two girls just stood there with a look of complete awe on their faces until he was out of sight.

Later that night, after the girls went to bed, Judy said to me in a quiet voice, "How did you pull that off? He was a great Santa."

"One of the guys at work is a Shriner, and for a $15 donation, Santa will come to your house and talk to your kids. It sure worked. They were shocked, weren't they."

"Ya done good, Daddy. Ya done good."

EPILOGUE

Christmas eve night was the usual battle of trying to get the excited girls to bed. My mother and father came over from Tampa to enjoy Christmas with us, and I'm glad they did. We finally got the girls to bed around 11, and Judy came out of the utility room with a kitchen set and a desk, and both had to be assembled. Great! My father and I waited an extra 30 minutes to make sure the girls were asleep before we tackled the kitchen set. As we opened the box, my Dad exclaimed, "This thing is metal!"

We unpacked all of the pieces and read through the instructions. I know, Dads aren't supposed to read instructions, but I'm glad we did. While my Dad laid out the pieces, I went to the toolbox and got the necessary tools. After 45 minutes of painful assembly, the kitchen was done. Judy passed out the band-aids to cover our cut fingers, and we attacked the desk.

Now, my father and I are fairly good at putting things together, but this desk almost beat us both. By two in the morning, we were stumped. With over half the desk assembled, we just could not get the sideboard to fit. After pouring over the instructions, we finally figured out that the sideboard had not been drilled. After another 30 minutes of measuring and drilling, the desk was finally done. While I put the tools away, my Dad carried the desk into the living room and placed it by the tree. My mother put a big bow on the top, and we all trudged off to bed at 3:30.

The kids woke us up at 6:30 with a roar of, "Get up. Get up. Santa came last night. After Judy and I got dressed we dragged ourselves into the living room. My Mom and Dad were already sitting on the couch looking just as bad as I'm sure we looked. With only three hours sleep it was hard to put on a happy face while the girls showed us their toys. As they paraded their treasures in front of us, I looked at my Dads face. Even though he was tired his face was aglow as I'm sure mine was. Watching Melissa at her new desk and Christie at her kitchen set we had both forgotten about our cut fingers and tired bodies as we watched their happy faces.

The Christmas Tree

Richard McNamara

Christmas is an exciting time for a five-year-old. The snow entices one to build snowmen and participate in snowball fights. Added to that is the thrill of sledding down the hill in the park at the end of the street. But all these things pale at the anticipation of seeing Santa Clause for the first time in my childhood memory.

I remember bundling up in my winter coat, mittens, and hat for a quick ride to where my mother worked. She led me into a large room filled with tables of cookies, candied apples, and popcorn balls. But the real thrill was standing in line with other kids and seeing Santa coming into the room with his sack of toys. After several minutes I was helped onto Santa's lap, where he asked, "And what would you like for Christmas, Richard?"

He even knew my name! I didn't remember that when we came into the room, a nice lady put a name tag on the front of my shirt.

"A new bicycle," I stammered.

"Ho, Ho, Ho," he chuckled. "Well. I'll see what I can do," he said in his deep, booming voice as he reached down into a huge pile of presents at his side. "But for now, here is a nice gift, and remember, I'm always watching. So be a good boy for your mother and father."

With another, "Ho, Ho, Ho," he helped me down, and I ran to my mother, clutching the present in my arms. "Did you tell Santa what you wanted for Christmas?"

"I sure did!" I said. "I told him I wanted a new bike."

"A new bike," my mother said. "What's wrong with the one you have now?"

"Aw. It's too small," I said. "And it's all messed up."

"Well. That's because you leave it outside instead of putting it in the garage like you're supposed to. I guess now it's up to Santa." Just before we left, my mother let me open Santa's gift. It was great! In the box were two shiny cap pistols with a double holster, just like the cowboys in the western shows. I strapped the belt around my waist, put the two guns in their holsters, and walked toward the door feeling "ten feet tall," as the saying goes. I was so proud of my new guns that I didn't notice that many other boys were sporting the same gift that I had received.

When my mother and I drove up in front of our house, we saw my dad's old Hudson parked at the curb. "Dad's home," I said, just a little too loud. "Maybe we can go get our Christmas tree."

"We'll see," my mother said. "He might be tired. You know he had to drive that special tour bus all day. We will just have to wait and see."

We hadn't even gotten through the door when I took off through the living room, yelling, "Dad. Dad. Look what Santa gave me," leaving a trail of gloves, hat, and coat as I went. "It's guns just like the cowboys have." I was almost to the end of the room when my dad came out of the kitchen with a sandwich in his hand.

"Guns, huh? Well. Let's see 'em," he said as he took another bite. When I handed him one of the pistols, he turned it over in his hand and told me, "Wow. That's a pretty sharp lookin' shootin' iron. Better be careful with that."

Handing the weapon back, I stuck it in the holster and, without taking a breath, I looked at him, "Can we go get a Christmas tree? If you're not too tired."

"No. I think we can do that. Go put on your coat and stuff, and we'll go see what we can find."

What we found was the most beautiful Christmas tree in the world. To my small eyes, it was huge. My dad and the tree guy tied it on top of my dad's car. It was so large it hung over front and rear. When we got home, I wanted to take it inside immediately, but my mother said that we had some furniture to move first, so I reluctantly walked into the house, constantly looking over my shoulder at the tree.

Once the few pieces of furniture were moved into the den, my father untied the tree from his car and drug it up onto the front porch. While I watched over the tree with my trusty guns at my side, my father went down to the basement to get the tree holder, and a saw to cut the bottom of the tree to fit. Once he was satisfied with his trimming, he attached the tree holder. After tightening the screws on the holder, we (I helped) pulled the big tree through the front door.

With the tree lying on the living room floor, we realized just how big it really was. With both my mom and dad wrestling with the tree, it was finally in place in front of the living room window for all to see. My dad laid down on the floor and readjusted the tree holder several times to make sure the tree stood straight, but it was finally done. Well, not really. Even with the high ceiling in our living room, the topmost branch touched the plaster. So, using the step stool from the kitchen, my dad had to take a pair of scissors and cut the branch off. While he was doing this, my mother brought boxes of lights and ornaments from the den. I was mesmerized as the lights transformed the plain green tree into the beginning of a beautiful Christmas tree.

While my dad continued to wind the strings of lights around the tree, my mother went into the kitchen to fix dinner. My dad had to drag me from my chair to the kitchen table when dinner was ready. As I wolfed my food down, I could see the tree through the living room door. "Whoa," my dad said as I stuffed food into my mouth. "I know you're excited about decorating the tree, but you need to slow down, or your gonna choke."

"Okay, Dad," I said through a mouthful of food. "But I just wanna get the tree decorated."

After we finished supper and my mother had cleared the table, we all went back to trim the tree. I placed ornaments on the branches until I couldn't reach them anymore. I went to the corner of the room, sat in my little rocker, and watched the transformation. It wasn't too long before all the boxes were empty. My father grabbed the step stool he had used before and put the angel on the top of the tree. It was the most beautiful tree I had ever seen. While I gawked at the shining ornaments and the glow of the lights, my mother came out of the den with boxes of tinsel. She and my father went around the tree, placing the shiny strips on every branch. When they finished, they sat on the sofa and gazed at the tree with smiles on their faces.

After a few minutes, my dad got up and turned all of the lights in the room off. The tree seemed to shimmer as the tree lights reflected off of the ornaments and the tinsel. We were all enjoying the peace and serenity of the moment when there was a slight noise from somewhere near the tree. My father had just started to get up from the sofa when the tree toppled over and crashed to the floor. The whole room was covered in broken ornaments and smashed light bulbs from the strings of lights. The angel slid across the floor and stopped right next to my small rocking chair. I slowly leaned over and picked it up with tears running down my cheeks.

But Where Will Santa Put Our Gifts?

Peggy Insula

When the time came to put our Christmas tree up, I had been on a long campaign to weed out items we no longer needed. Housekeeping is hard enough for people who aren't clutter bugs, let alone for those of us who can't resist collecting shiny things. I find no joy in cleaning and dusting, and I have arrived at the time of life when I need to dispose of what I've already acquired. My goal is to own as few things as possible before I die.

I approached my husband, otherwise known as the Cherisher of Material Objects. He grew up in Cuba with nothing but four flimsy walls, a moody ocean, and all the sand he could ever want, so I made every effort to be gentle. "Listen up, Fidel," I said. "We're too damn old to be climbing on step ladders to put up trees. There are three clogging up the closet: one five-footer and two tabletop sizes. I'm throwing the big one out."

He turned on me with an expression I'd seen once when I dumped a bucket of mop water over his head. "No. I'll put that tree up. It's not that hard." He turned and walked away. End of discussion.

I sighed and went to the kitchen to read the expiration dates on about a zillion cans of vegetables.

The very next day, he put up the largest tree. It fit on our dining table as long as he wedged the angel on top tightly against the ceiling. A climbing cat could have pulled it down, but luckily, we didn't have one.

Now, my problem was that Eugenio had put up the tree before I had a chance to ask him to move the table it sat on.

I approached him again. "Eugenio, you know I can't move furniture since I broke my back in seven places. I need you to move the table with the tree. Actually, just turn it ninety degrees, so we have room to lean back the recliner seats on the couch. Right now, one recliner bumps into the bookcase. You complained about that a day or so ago. Remember?"

He kept watching the hockey game. "The table's all right where it is. I already put up the tree."

"The tree won't be hard to manage. All we have to do is take the angel off the top and set the tree on the floor. We can put it back when the table is moved."

"No. I told you the tree is okay."

I'm ashamed to admit that at times I don't accept the word "no" with much grace. In fact, I plain don't take "no" for an answer when my mind is set on something. "Never give up" is a virtue, isn't it? Anyway, I searched for a response to motivate him to comply. Hmm. My birthday was the next day, and he has always treated my birthday like a holy day. He showers me with whatever gifts I want, including flowers and candy, and puts himself at my beck and call all day. I could have just waited until the next day, and he would have bent over backwards to move that table for me. But I was in a snit. I stomped into the bedroom and yelled, "Oh, yeah? Well, you can just forget about celebrating my birthday tomorrow." I slammed the door and left him sitting in the living room. You won't find finely tuned manipulative actions such as this described in marriage manuals. You have to learn them on the job, so to speak. Pity.

Arms crossed, I sat on the bed and fumed. In a few minutes, noises from the living room suggested that Eugenio was up and moving furniture. I listened until all was quiet again before re-entering the living room. When I did, Eugenio sat on the couch. The table was moved where I wanted it. But where was the tree?

"Thank you, Eugenio," I said. "Where's the tree?"

"In the dumpster."

Aha. He wanted to punish me. So, I said, "Good. Now we'll have more space in the closet."

When he didn't reply, I hummed "We wish you a merry Christmas" and arranged the table cloth. Then I looked around for the smaller trees. "Eugenio, where are the two little trees?"

He didn't even look away from the hockey game. "In the dumpster."

"What! You threw those away too?"

"Yes. We're not having Christmas trees this year."

No use responding to that. I stared at the two boxes of ornaments that waited on a chair. I wondered if I should throw those out too.

The next day, Eugenio was as eager to celebrate my birthday as ever. He bought my favorite cake, a Christmassy bouquet, and a perfect card. He fixed my favorite steak and salad.

At the end of the day, he asked, "How was your birthday?"

"Almost perfect."

"What would make it perfect?"

"You owe me a goddam Christmas tree.

The Christmas Coon Hound

Peggy Insula

Whimpering woke me from the dancing sugarplums way too early on Christmas morning. Did one of the kids have a bellyache from too many cookies? No, the groaning wasn't human. I sprang from my bed to see what the matter was.

My three kids beat me to the living room. They didn't even notice me while they sat under the huge, glittering, real pine tree and stroked a furry animal, whose long tail flapped on the floor.

The whining had stopped. A short-haired, floppy eared, red pup lay on her back and soaked in the caresses and adoration of my gob smacked children.

Wrapping paper and ribbons littered the floor all around. The pup was entangled in red and green satin strands—probably couldn't move more than her tail. One of the presents she had opened was a pair of leather gloves for twelve-year-old Valerie, the oldest. One glove was in pristine shape; the other had been chewed to a fare-the-well—what was left of it, that is, since the pup had evidently eaten a few fingers.

I stooped to pick up the unchewed glove, but it was stuck to the carpet with part of a slobbery candy cane. Closer inspection of the carpet and the tree revealed that all the candy canes within puppy reach had been partially consumed and stuck to the carpet in a random pattern that failed to amuse me much. "What in the world was Santa thinking?"

Three heads swiveled to stare at me with identical wide, blue eyes. Travis, my nine-year-old, exclaimed, "She's beautiful! She's the best present ever!"

The other two nodded enthusiastically. The puppy grunted and flapped her tail harder while the four-year-old, Wheat, exchanged sloppy kisses with her.

Clearly, no more presents would be opened for the moment. I thanked God for Florida's temperate winter weather and shooed the kids and the pup into the back yard. I was filling a trash bag with shredded paper and tangled ribbons when my husband, Eugene, sauntered in with a big yawn and a cup of coffee. "Did I miss the fun?" he asked.

I rolled my eyes at him. "I think the fun has just begun with that devil dog. Look what she did to the tree, the carpet, Valerie's gloves—"

A guffaw from Eugene cut me off. Poking around behind the tree, he held up a strange, roughly rectangular object that might have been a large, dark brick. He turned it in his hands to give me a look at the gnawed end. "At last we have someone who appreciates Aunt June's yearly fruitcake offering," he said.

"No wonder the poor critter was crying like she had a stomach ache."

We were sniffing at a suspicious wet spot on the trunk of the Christmas tree when out on the lawn arose a great clatter. Eugene and I looked at each other in alarm and made haste to the back yard. A garbage can lid had been tied to the pup with some of her ribbons, and she was happily banging her way across the patio to the howling delight of my husband's children.

"You deal with them," I said. The Christmas coon hound was your big idea. How much eggnog did you drink before you decided to shop for a pup?"

Eugene hung his head. "She begged me to take her with those sad puppy eyes. She's just like the dogs in Where the Redfern Grows. How could I resist her?" He took his coffee and went out into the fray.

I stood at the window to check on his progress. In his red and green plaid robe and rumpled black hair, he looked like a deranged Scotsman. The kids were clad in their loud Christmas jammies, too. Wheat clapped his chubby hands, jumped up and down, and shrieked with every pass of the goofy pup. The neighbors were in for quite a show this morning. I sighed and headed to the kitchen to check on the turkey. Eugene and I were going to have to have a serious talk, or maybe an all-out fist fight, about managing that hound.

That evening after dinner, the creature was stirring all through the house and seeking what she could turn over and/or destroy. So far, every trash can was upended, and toilet paper streamed out of the bathroom and down the hall into the living room. The kids were filled with glee at Gator Bait's tricks. (I christened her that because part of me—okay, a big part— hoped she might wander into a nearby pond and mysteriously disappear. Bad, bad Scrooge mama!)

When at last the children were nestled all snug in their beds, I called Eugene on the carpet—on one of the few spots not candy-cane sticky. "Listen, Christmas Goose," I said. "You do realize that this pup is a hunting dog, not a house pet, don't you?"

He stared at his feet and pulled toilet paper off his left reindeer slipper. "I'm sure she'll adapt.

The kids will train her and take care of her."

My plum pudding jaw dropped to the sticky carpet. "You mean those kids who wouldn't pick up their own rooms with the help of Mary Poppins and a magic wand? Those kids who think bathing and brushing their teeth are cruel and unusual punishments? Those kids who have never demonstrated that they know the difference between inside and outside of a trash can? What makes you think they won't teach the dog more bad habits?"

Eugene rubbed his chin and lay a finger aside of his nose. He gave a nod. "Hmmm. Well, maybe it won't be easy, but we need to give Beast a chance."

I sighed and clasped my hands to keep from strangling him. "Oh, so you admit she's a beast.

You have two weeks to show some progress with that hound from Hell. I'm not cleaning after her. If she isn't adapting, we'll have to place her with a nice, gullible farmer who is plagued with coons."

"Yes, dear."

I stomped off, and that night, I in my kerchief and he in his cap, we settled our brains with our backs to each other through the long winter's nap.

The next morning, the stockings that had been hung by the chimney with care were strewn throughout the house and meticulously chewed and shredded. I spoke not a word but turned straight to my task of making blueberry pancakes and sausage while my husband and kids removed the evidence that Gator Bait had not, alas, spent her night contemplating the moon on the breast of the new fallen snow.

We had breakfast, and then in a twinkling, I rounded on the kids and the pup and said, "Now dash away! Dash away! Dash away all!"

They all flew outside like the down of a thistle.

Peace reigned in the house while I cleaned the kitchen...until a loud thumping drew me to the window like a flash. I tore open the shutters and threw up the sash. It took me only seconds to locate the noise. What to my wondering eyes should appear? Leaping to the top of the porch, to the top of the wall, that crazy dog chased tennis balls thrown by the kids. She had two in her mouth, stretching her merry dimples flat, and was trying to pick up a third. I shook my head and paused to gaze at my children. The kids' eyes—how they twinkled! I laughed when I saw them in spite of myself.

From the open window, I drew in my head and was turning around when a ball, as stray as a dry leaf before a wild hurricane, met with an obstacle and crashed through the other window. I stomped to the living room where Eugene stood gazing into a half-filled trash bag. He looked like a peddler just opening his sack. He turned a startled stare on me.

I placed my hands on my hips, and with my fiercest expression, gave him to know he had something to dread. "Your children and that foolish hound are destroying the house. What do you intend to do about it?"

"Aw, honey. You can't blame the dog. It's the children who need training." He shot me an annoying wink of his eye and twist of his head, opened the outside door, whistled, and shouted, and called his children by name: "Now! Valerie, now! Travis, now! Wheat, now!"

More rapid than eagles, those children, they came. Wheat brought up the rear, his droll little mouth drawn up like a bow. "Please, Dad, we didn't mean to do it." Tears ran down his cheeks that were like roses and his nose like a cherry.

Eugene sighed. "I know, I know. Come in and settle down. We'll talk about it."

A family council convened around the dining table. Gator Bait soon tired of the inactivity and slinked off to the living room. Engrossed in discussion, none of us noticed.

Eugene's hands were folded on the table. He leaned forward. "Kids, you know that Beast is on probation here for two weeks. So far, her chances of staying look slim. Your mother will not tolerate deconstruction of our home." He shot me a wimpy-eyed glance.

Shamefaced, the children hung their heads. From under the table, little feet pranced and pawed.

Valerie spoke first. "We'll pay for the window. You can take it out of our allowances or our college funds."

The boys nodded.

"Look," I said. "I'm giving Gator Bait a fair chance, but you kids need to take responsibility for her at all times. By the way, where is she now?"

Heads turned. Chairs scraped and fell over as we leapt to our feet, dashed away to the living room, and stopped short. No dog. Just a mouse or something stirring in the chimney.

We stared at each other in wonder until down the chimney Gator Bait came with a bound. Her coat was all tarnished with ashes and soot. She shook her floppy ears in a cloud of black dust that encircled her head like a wreath, trotted over to us, and proudly dropped a writhing squirrel at our feet.

"Look, Mom," Travis said. "She's ridding our house of vermin."

Eugene's little round belly shook when he laughed, like a bowl full of jelly.

I glared at him. "I don't see anything funny."

"You must admit," Eugene said, "the pup is trying to please."

"You guys clean the living room and give the dog a bath. I'll call a window repairman." I stomped back to the kitchen, made the call, and sat grumbling into my coffee cup.

As the days slowly passed, the chances of my acceptance of Gator Bait dwindled like the luster of midday. She acted exactly like...a hound dog. I told my family to prepare themselves for placing Gator Bait in a good, bad, or indifferent home.

Then one afternoon a frightening event took place. I was washing dishes and gazing out the window. The children and the dog were playing catch on the front lawn. The ball rolled into the road in front of a little old driver, so lively and quick. What happened next stopped my heart.

Wheat ran heedlessly into the road in front of the car. I dropped a dish and shrieked. Black dread engulfed me. Brakes squealed. Like a flash, Gator Bait bounded between the car and my child, grabbed Wheat by his pants, and dragged him away from the car and onto the grass.

I clung to the edge of the sink and tried to stop moaning as the driver, his beard as white as the snow and the stump of a pipe held tight in his teeth, emerged from the car and tottered toward Wheat and Gator Bait.

Eugene tore out of the side yard and rushed to the scene. I was not far behind. We dropped to our knees and threw our arms around Wheat and the smiling hound.

The little old man waddled closer. "Is the boy all right?"

Wheat, wide-eyed and speechless, just nodded.

Eugene caught his breath. "It's not your fault."

"No," I agreed, "and I'll never, ever let this precious dog go."

Happy Christmas to all, and to all a good night!

Christmas Blizzard

Nancy Clark

Sadie paced back and forth at the baggage pickup area; she was waiting for her parents, whose flight just arrived from Arizona.

She hadn't seen them in six months. Since she left home for college in July.

They were coming to spend Christmas with her in Indiana. They hadn't seen snow in ten years and were excited to learn it would be a white Christmas!

Her dad spotted her first, "Sadie Doodle." Making his way to her, he lifted her off the floor, kissed her on the cheek, then put her down.

Walking up to them, her mother pulled in for a long hug. "It's been too long since we've seen you," she said with a smile.

"I know. Mom. But you're here now and I have some exciting things planned! Let's get your luggage and head to the apartment.

Once the suitcases were retrieved and put in the car they set out for Sadie's place.

The drive took about a half hour. Sadie asked how their flight was. They had a story to tell about the little girl who sat in front of them. She was just too cute for words and kept playing peek-a-boo with them.

After arriving at the apartment, Sadie showed them to their room. " I know how tiring long flights are, do you want to take a short nap before supper?" she asked.

"Sounds like a great idea, I am a bit worn out," her Dad said. Her Mom agreed.

"Sleep well, I'll wake you about a half hour before dinner, so you can freshen up," she told them as she closed the door.

Sadie headed out to the kitchen to prepare her parents favorite dish, Chicken Marsala. Preparations took an half an hour. While the dish simmered, she busied herself by making a nice tossed salad.

When everything was about ready, she knocked on the guest room door, saying,

"Anybody hungry?"

Her Dad rubbed his eyes and sniffed the air, "Something smells mighty good."

Nudging his wife, "Hey, sleepy head, I heard dinner's ready, and the aroma is divine. So, get a hustle in your giddy-up, I'm starved."

Smiling she responded, "Yes dear, whatever you say."

They sat down at the dining table to enjoy the Chicken Marsala, Sadie had made. After clearing the dishes, she brought out a dessert of Tiramisu.

"Dear, that was a most excellent meal," her dad said.

"Yes indeed. the Tiramisu was so moist and tasted like a bit of heaven," her mother added.

Blushing slightly she thanked them both.

They adjourned to the living room to chat a bit and watch the news.

Looking over at her Dad she saw his eyes were starting to droop.

Standing up to stretch, Sadie said, "It's been a long day, I think it's time to hit the hay. I want to take you on a tour of the area tomorrow and I am sure we all have some shopping to do."

Her parents agreed, they all hugged each other and said their goodnights.

The next day dawned, the sun was up, and it was just starting to snow.

Sadie had breakfast ready when her parents got up around 9:00. She made a coffeecake and had a pot of coffee brewed.

"I hope you slept well," she said as they walked into the kitchen.

"I think I was asleep before my head hit the pillow," her dad said laughing.

Her Mom added, "I slept like a log, except your Dad was snoring logs!"

They enjoyed a leisurely breakfast before getting dressed to take a drive around the town.

She took them to the Studebaker museum first, which her dad loved and didn't want to leave. He made sure to get a tee-shirt and a couple of baseball hats.

Asking them if they wouldn't mind taking a walk in the cold, she wanted to take them to Mishawaka Riverwalk. Both said that sound like fun and didn't mind the chill in the air.

Along the walk they stopped at a picnic table to enjoy some hot chocolate Sadie had remembered to bring.

Their final stop was a tour of the school she was going to. It was a lovely campus, tree lined walkways, with wide open space decorated with sculptures made by students.

On the way back to Sadie's apartment the snow started coming down heavier and was sticking to the ground.

The following day they all bundled up to go get a Christmas tree and then do some shopping for presents. After decorating the tree, their Christmas presents were placed under everything looked fabulous.

Christmas was two days away and the weather forecasters were predicting there would be plenty of snow to have a white Christmas.

Sadie's parents were overjoyed to hear the news.

On Christmas Eve it was snowing; her parents put on their heavy coats, mittens, and hats and went outside. They were like two little kids, throwing snowballs at each other, making snow angels, and finally a pair of snowmen.

Sadie made sure to capture their playfulness by taking pictures with her iPhone while she stood on the porch watching.

"Okay, you two, it's time to come out of the cold, You've been out here long enough. I don't want you to catch a cold," she shouted.

"Come on in and let's have some hot chocolate.

"Yes, mom we're coming just when we were having fun," her mom chuckled.

"She is such an old worry wart, isn't she" her dad added. He made a quick snowball and tossed it at his daughter, it hit her on the right shoulder.

Laughing she gathered some snow from the porch and sent a snowball flying at her dad, hitting him the chest. Everyone trudged into the house to warm up with some hot chocolate.
As the day progressed the winds picked up and snow was coming down faster and heavier.

Turning on the news they found out that there was a winter storm warning issued for the area. The weather person said they were expecting eight to ten inches of snow, drifts, and high winds. He also advised people to stay off the roads due to poor driving conditions.

"Wow, did you put a request in for all this snow?" her Dad kidded.

"Nope, not my idea! Well, if we do lose power during this we have no worries this complex has a generator," Sadie replied.

Christmas dawned with the wind still blowing, it was almost a whiteout as they weren't able to make out Sadie's car in the parking lot.

So, they just settled and opened Christmas presents, having a wonderful time in each other's company ignoring the world outside.

No Christmas With Aunt Holly

Nancy Clark

We got the news, that Aunt Holly had passed away on July 1st.

This took the clan by surprise as she was so spry and healthy at then last get together.

Aunt Holly was the chief planner for all the family events. It gave her so much pleasure and made her feel useful.

Her husband, Uncle Rudy, had passed away several years back leaving her a nice nest egg to live out the rest of her life in comfort.

Aunt Holly's passing was exactly halfway to Christmas and the day she would always start planning the festivities.

Funeral arrangements were made. The service was to be held at the East Methodist church where she and Uncle Rudy were married, Reverend Hatch along with Reverend Nesmith would conduct the ceremony. The church was packed, as Aunt Holly was well loved by everyone in town.

A private gravesite ceremony was held for the family and her two dearest friends Chelsea and Simone.

When we arrived back at her house, it was full of well-wishers, who had brought in all kinds of various goodies. Everyone reminisced how Aunt Holly would do this or how she did that. It was nice to hear how much she had touched so many in the community.

Slowly, everyone departed and we were alone, the house was very still. No one spoke for some time.

Mom, Aunt Holly's sister finally broke the silence, "Who is going to do all the planning for Christmas this year? I have no idea where to even begin. Holly planned everything, every little detail right down to where each ornament should be hung," she sobbed.

Dad came over and knelt in front of her, "Mary, let's not worry about that right now. Let's just wait a few days, give ourselves sometime for this all to calm down. There is still plenty of time."

"You're right, Noel, as always. Okay, I think it is time for us all to get some rest. It has been a very long week. To bed everyone." Mom decreed. "Good night kids see you in the morning."

"Night, Mom, Dad," both of them said at the same time. "Sleep well, we love you," Each kissing their parents before heading upstairs.

Mary and Noel followed after making sure the house was secure and all the lights were out.

Carol got up early the next morning and soon the house was filled with the smells of freshly brewed coffee and coffeecake.

"Something smells mighty good," her Dad said as he rubbed his eyes. He wandered over kissed his daughter, and then poured himself a cup of coffee.

"Morning, I couldn't sleep any longer so I figured why not get up and fix us all something to eat. I know there is a lot of food here already, but I wanted to, well you know."

"Yes, dear, I understand and I am sure your Mom will be happy."

"Did I just hear something about Mom being happy?"

"Morning, Mom! I made your favorite coffeecake. Come sit down have a slice and I will get you some coffee," Carol said pulling a chair out for her.

"Honey, it smells wonderful and thank you."

"What is with all the noise down here! Can't a guy get any sleep?" Chris remarked as he strolled into the kitchen. "Wait a minute, Carol baked something? Is it safe to eat? You know how she. . ."

Carol threw a towel at her younger brother, "Shut up, sit down and eat! Let me get you some milk. Would you rather have some cold cereal?"

"Nah, I will live dangerously today," he replied laughing.

As they ate, they went over the plans for the upcoming two weeks. Mary was appointed as the executor for the estate so she had a full plate ahead of her. One thing for certain, the house would not be sold; it was the center for all Christmas festivities. There was plenty of room for the entire family to stay.

For the rest of the day would just be a day of relaxation and reminiscing. There were so many wonderful memories of Aunt Holly.

The following week they started the process of sorting everything out. Carol would take care of the study, Chris the attic, Mary her sister's bedroom and Noel the garage.

Before heading to the garage Noel, stopped and questioned Mary, "What do you want to do with the SUV? It's in great shape and there aren't too many miles on it. If I recall she just got in two years ago and never really drove it anywhere."

"I think we should donate it to her favorite charity, *Helping Feed the Hungry*. I am sure they could put it to good use."

"A perfect solution, I'll give them a call now to let them know," he said kissing her on the cheek. He reached for the Aunt Holly's phone directory to search for their number.

"Let's meet back down here in about two hours for updates on anything we find. Is that okay with everyone?"

Thumbs up went around the kitchen.

Mary headed to her sister's bedroom, Chris wandered upstairs to beginning to go through stuff in the attic, and Carol headed down the hall into the study. When Noel finished his call, he entered the garage.
Time slowly clicked by, when suddenly, Carol shouted, "Everyone get in here quick, I found something!"

Everyone came running into the study. They all shouted, "What?"

Smiling, she held up a green and red tartan notebook. It was embossed with the words *Christmas Must Go Forward.*

"Mom, I think Aunt Holly somehow knew she wouldn't be around to get everything set-up this year! She left us this so we could do it!"

"Carol, I think you're right," she said as she lovingly touched the cover.

Opening the notebook they scanned through the book. Each page showed pictures of various parts of the house.

The first one was of the front door, with a photo of the wreath that was to be hung on it. Another showed the staircase with a detailed explanation of how she wanted the garland draped along it with decorative lights. Further into the book was the fireplace, again with her vision of how it should be adorned.

Finally, the last was of a Christmas tree. In the description of her vision she had written, *"This year I know I won't be with you, I want you to use your imagination while putting the decorations in place. Use all of your knowledge of what I have done in the past. Make this tree one of honor. Know that I love you and will be with you in spirt. All my love, Aunt Holly."*

After looking through all the pictures they were all in tears.

Noel spoke first, "We will honor Holly with a truly remarkably decorated tree. It will be the best Christmas tree this family has ever had!"

Chris seconded the idea, "I found some antique decoration in the attic. I know she had never used them on our trees before. They would be perfect." Carol and Mary nodded in agreement.

The following week they headed home. Months passed by quickly, each on spent with plans for Christmas Day.

On December 1st, they set out to Aunt Holly's house to begin turning it into a holiday tribute to Holly. Every detail she wanted for the main decorations was found and placed with care.

As was the family custom, they headed out on Christmas Eve to cut down a tree in the forest near the house. They found the perfect one, seven feet tall, nice and full. Tying in to the roof of the car, they headed back, singing carols all the way.

Chris had brought all of the decoration from the attic down the day before. Lights were added. Then gently they unwrapped decorations and hung them on the tree. Mary took the delicate Christmas angel and with help from Noel, she placed it atop the tree.

Carol plugged the lights in and they all stood back.

The tree looked amazing. It truly had Aunt Holly's personage all over it. With tears in their eyes they hugged each other.

Noel excused himself and asked Chris to follow him out to the garage.

"I wonder what he is up to," Mary wondered aloud.

"Dad is a man of many surprises."

"That is true."

Noel and Chris came back into the room their hands full of brightly decorated planters of Christmas Holly in full bloom. They carefully placed them around the tree.

"Noel, what a lovely idea," Mary said quietly with tears rolling down her face. "Holly is definitely in this room."

The next day the entire family arrived and all remarked on how beautifully decorated the tree was.

Christmas was tough that year but everyone felt Aunt Holly was with them.

Christmas is My Secret Lover

Holly Schwartztol

Through the decades, I've had to deny this passion, stuffing it down amid Chanukah candles and appropriate holiday behaviors. My family was Jewish, and we celebrated both Jewish and other holidays.

But my early childhood was filled with all things Christmas. Each year, on Christmas Eve, we'd go to one of many street corners on the upper west side of New York City to select the best tree and then lug it home through often icy streets. Inevitably, the tree would be a bit lopsided or too tall and adjustments had to be made. My mother and brother typically did the actual setting up, placing the tree in a bucket to keep it moist and then placing the lights on the tree. Often, one or two lights were faulty and necessitated replacement.

The trees in those years were true evergreens and, as I breathe in now, the scent of pine needles filling the apartment triggers so many recollections. Then, my best friend, Lily Hirschel, would come over as the two of us were chosen to decorate the tree. Her family was much more religious, so she couldn't have a tree herself.

The boxes of ornaments were brought down from closets. So many still linger in my memory. The cottony Santas, the sparkly balls, tiny birds all were familiar friends just bursting to be placed on the tree branches. A white cottony skirt with sparkles was placed at the bottom of the tree. An adult always placed the top ornament on the tree. When all the branches were laden with decorations, Lily and I had the joy of tossing tinsel onto the tree.

But Christmas was much more than just the tree. When I was very little, I went to my Aunt and Uncle's and we all sang Christmas carols through the streets of their neighborhood near Columbia University.

I'd go to sleep on Christmas eve full of anticipation of Christmas morning when my brother, Michael, and I woke our parents up as early as possible. Sometimes, before Christmas, I'd spy wrapped packages in the coat closet and try to guess what was in them. Funny, sometimes the packages themselves were more fun than the actual gifts inside.

Usually, we'd go for Christmas lunch at my grandparents who we called Nanny and Os (Nanny who didn't want to be called grandma and Os, because his name was Osmond and everyone called him Os.) They lived in a brownstone on West 11th street in Greenwich Village. Classical music emanated from the record player. A grand piano faced the windows. Os and Nanny lived on the main floor and the basement. They rented the two upper floors to a tenant. I never actually saw that apartment. I think my parents were married there in 1934.

The long wooden table downstairs with delicate, China plates and thick cobalt blue goblets were filled with delicious foods and drink. Sometimes, as the youngest child, I'd get a bit restless with all the formality, but the delicious aromas fill my senses even now.

The smell of pine, the crunch and stickiness of candy canes, the twinkling of lights, the warmth of family all mixed together with sounds of The First Noel and O Little Town of Bethlehem evoke sweetness all through my being. My secret lover lies forever within me.

A Favorite Christmas Memory

Kay Williamson

Many years ago, around Christmas, I had this conversation with Diane, my six year old sister. I was six years older, at the time, and approaching my teenage years.

"Kay, I don't believe in Santa Claus anymore," Diane announced to me one morning.

"Oh? So who do you think leaves all those nice presents under the Christmas tree?"

"Mother and Daddy play Santa Claus."

"Oh, really? Diane, where did you get that idea?"

"Cousin Jane told me."

Why was I not surprised? Cousin Jane was nine years old. Diane was too young not to be a believer. I had to think fast. "So, I've always been told that Santa would not leave any presents if you stopped believing in him," I told the disbeliever. "Do you want to take a chance on not getting any presents?"

Diane looked a bit troubled. "Well do YOU still believe in Santa Claus?"

"Of course," I lied. "I still get presents, don't I?"

"Well, I don't know. It does seem strange that Santa can go all over the world in one night."

"Yes, I agree, but he's magic. And it's possible that he has a lot of magic helpers."

"I don't know. I'll have to think about it."

Patting her on her head I said, "Okay, you do that." I turned away knowing that I had to have some reinforcements. Since it was Saturday, I knew my daddy would soon be home from his early morning fishing trip.

A short time later, I heard him entering the front door so I ran to meet him.

"Guess what, Daddy? Diane told me she didn't believe in Santa Claus anymore. And you might know that Cousin Jane was the little 'knower all' who spilled the beans. Diane thinks you and Mother are the ones who put the presents under the tree."

Daddy shook his head and grinned. "Well, I think we can keep her believing for at least one more year. Let me think about it."

I felt relieved because Christmas had never been the same since I had stopped being a believer.

The following week was Christmas Eve. I was hopeful and excited when Daddy had revealed his plan. At that time, Diane and I shared the same bedroom and bed. Daddy was to pick up fallen black walnuts from our tree and then throw the walnuts on our tin roof. Diane would want to know what the noise was.

Fast forward to Christmas Eve. Diane and I were in the bed when the noise started on top of the roof. As we expected, Diane sat up in bed and whispered, "What is that noise?" "I guess it's Santa. You'd better pretend you're asleep if you want him to leave you any presents."

My little sister fell back into bed and pulled the covers over her head. "You'd better also pretend you're asleep, or he might not leave YOU any presents," she mumbled.

So that's how my daddy and I kept Diane believing for a few more years. I did have a firm talk with Cousin Jane, and told her not to divulge any more information about Santa.

After all these years, it's still one of our favorite Christmas memories.

Author Biographies

Christopher Robin Adams

Christopher Robin Adams has been published from England to Hawaii since 1958. He is Vice President of the Space Coast Writers Guild and President of Scribblers, a Brevard County writing group. Spanish Cedar, *Preserving the ART of the Cigar Experience*, is his first poetry collection. He is also published in the Brevard Scribblers' Anthologies: *Driftwood* and *Written in the Sun*.

UCF Florida Writing Project/Mentor www.nwp.org
https://www.facebook.com/christopher.adams.5454021
Spanish Cedar Website: www.spanishcedarbook.com

Peggy Downey Ball

Peggy Downey Ball is originally from New York and Connecticut. Her poetry, essays, and stories have appeared in *Golden Years* magazine, *Motor Boating and Sailing, Florida Today, Driftwood* and *Written in the Sun*. She has received awards from several local writers' clubs, and the National League of Pen Women. She has published five books of her work: *Tickle Toe Hill*; *The Many Moods of Love*; *50-50, the Mini Saga Book*; *Florida Souvenir*; and *What Do You Wish For*?

Nancy Clark

Nancy Clark has been writing since she was in second grade. Her first poem, published when she was only eight years old, featured in her school's literary book: *The Treasure Chest*. She has published four books: *Haiku for You*; *Haikus and Cinquains*; *Mini Sagas – Fifty Words or Bust,* and *Rainy-Day Reads*. As a member of The Scribblers of Brevard, she has had several of her short stories and poems published in their yearly anthology, *Driftwood* and *Written in The Sun*.

David Clark

After serving a 21-year career in the US Army, David earned his AA Degree from Brevard Community College; while there he served as Entertainment Editor for The Capsule, the school's newspaper. He then attended Rollins College on a scholarship to earn his Bachelor of Arts in English. David was ultimately accepted to and awarded the Rollins' Master of Liberal Studies program, in 2013. He went on to serve as an Instructor of English and Humanities at Eastern Florida Community College until 2021. Under the nom-de-plume Wickett d'Orion, he is the author of the New Dawn Trilogy [*New Dawn, Return of the Uk-Duk*, and *Here There & Elsewhere*].

Gloria I Colache

Gloria was born in Colombia. She moved to the United States in 1980, and worked as an accounting secretary for the New York City Public School for almost twenty years. Since 2003 she has lived in Melbourne, Florida. She has written a cookbook "Starts by hand". She is a member of Scribblers and was published in the *Driftwood* anthology in 2017. She loves to write, read and cook.

Anne-Marie Derouault

Born in Paris, living in Florida, Anne-Marie Derouault is a consultant in leadership, communication, and stress reduction, with a lifelong passion for mindfulness and yoga. She writes free verse poetry in English and French inspired by her love of travel, nature, and human beings. Anne-Marie has been published in several of the Brevard Scribblers' Anthologies.

Peggy Insula

Peggy Insula has published novels: *Letters to Uncle Jeb, Murder Runs in my Family,* and *Choices;* and novellas: *Just Murder, Sudsy, How Not to Steal a Car,* and *You're Nobody Till Somebody Kills You. Waiting Rooms* recounts her husband's cancer diagnosis and treatment. Fictional characters and events add humor to this otherwise daunting journey. *Chamomile Poems, Travels with Ninny and Zander, All the Dogs I've Loved Before,* and three anthologies complete her works.

Nick Kaplan

Nicholas Kaplan has published several short stories on life events and politics. Retired, he has written articles for The Scribblers of Brevard Anthologies: *Driftwood*, *Written in the Sun* and *Christmas 2021*. He is a member of the Space Coast Writers Guild and has contributed to The Anthology Alliance publications *Pandemic*, *PETS* and *Aftermath*. His self-published novel (under the nom de plume of Nicholas Taylor) entitled *The Long Game* is a 21st century story of espionage and government corruption.

Elayne Kershaw

After moving to Florida, British-born Elayne first wrote articles for local magazines before concentrating on fiction. Her short stories have been published several anthologies. This success led to acceptance into the League of American Pen Women as an International Writer. She is currently writing a collection of short stories about human relationships in the digital age. She is also an artist, photographer, and scuba diver. Her YouTube Channel, *Mediterranean Blue Films*©, showcases her underwater art films.

https://www.elaynesart.co.uk
https://www.facebook.com/elaynesart
https://www.youtube.com/c/mediterraneanbluefilms/playlists

Lou Kicha

Louis P Kicha is a retired dentist, married to Fern and living in Malabar with his dog, Remy and five cats. He worked for the State of Florida as Dental Director of St Johns County in St Augustine. He owned private practices in Indialantic and Melbourne and finished his career as a civilian dentist for the US Army at Joint Base Lewis-McChord in Tacoma, Washington. His hobbies include writing, scuba diving, underwater photography, traveling. He is a member of Scribblers of Brevard and the Florida Writers Association. He has published *The Deadly Ocean* (2016), *The Baikal Incident* (2019), and *Permafrost Eruption* (2020) all on Amazon.

Richard McNamara

Richard's interest in literature and writing goes back to his earliest years. His parents taught him to read at an early age, and he hasn't stopped reading yet! He is a collector of first editions, mainly Florida mystery writers, and he attends several writers' conferences every year. During his Electrical Engineering career, he wrote many technical articles and papers, and he used that experience to move into the field of writing fiction. He is published in several of the Brevard Scribbler's Anthologies and recently won third place in their 2021 Writing Competition.

Carolyn Newby

Carolyn has been a Resident of Eau Gallie for sixty-one years. She writes poetry, short fiction, and nonfiction. She loves the First Church of Melbourne, family, the beach, gardening, and Scribblers. Other interests are reading, bowling, music, and Gator football. Widowed after sixty years of marriage she has four children, five grandchildren and ten greats. She has enjoyed travel nationwide and to other countries, but her favorite place is here at home.

Linda Paul

Linda Paul is a writer and musician in Melbourne, Florida. Her monologue *Semper Fi* was performed on stage and TV in Portland, Oregon and her play *Christmas in the ICU* was a finalist in the Midwest Dramatists Center Conference 2018. She writes songs, plays, poems, essays and stories and teaches ukulele at the library. She has been *published in The Oregonian and the Brevard Scribblers* Driftwood Anthology. She is currently working on her first novel.

Holly W. Schwarztol Ph.D.

Holly is a poet, novelist, essayist, teacher, retired psychologist and a spiritual medium. She has written and published three novels and a book of poetry. Her fictional characters lead the narrative of her novels and her poems nearly fall out of her. Holly teaches memoir writing on zoom and has a waiting list for these classes. Her psychology and spiritual studies inform her writing about the intricacies of human relationships and the continuation of consciousness.

Dakota Williams

Dakota was assigned a task in sixth grade to create a Christmas story. *When Rudolph Got His Chance* was the result.

Kay Williamson

Kay writes murder mystery novels with a touch of romantic suspense. They include *Ghostly Whispers, Bridge to Nowhere, Listen to the Heart, Time After Time, Murder at the Starlight Pavilion, The Mysterious Woman on the Train, Incident at the Pink Beach House, Murder on Star Route 1, Murder in the Mountains* and Murder at the Reginal Hospital. Kay is an award-winning artist and a musician, composer, and playwright who has produced three albums: *Dreamflight, Magical Moments,* and *Gonna Love All Those Hurts.* Her romantic musical comedy, *What's Going on at the Mansion*, was produced in Iron Mountain, MI. Kay's books are available at Amazon.com and Barnes & Noble online. www.kaywilliamson.com.

Made in the USA
Columbia, SC
28 February 2023

13074052R00115